LLANILLTUD

It is difficult to imagine that Llanilltud Fawr was in the late fifth and early sixth centuries probably host to one of Britain's earliest centres of learning. It is also difficult to believe that a scholarly and critical in-depth study of such an important site has not been attempted before. This book has now plugged that gap splendidly.

THE MOST REVD DR BARRY MORGAN,
ARCHBISHOP OF WALES 2003–2017

Philip Morris takes us on a pilgrimage through the ages and generations of Llanilltud, using sound scholarship, careful research and a deep understanding of Celtic tradition. Crucially, by applying this pragmatically to popular traditions of Illtud's legacy, he reveals a deeper and more authentic inheritance, which informs the pilgrim journey of today.

THE REVD CANON EDWIN COUNSELL,
RECTOR OF LLANTWIT MAJOR

LLANILLTUD

The story of a Celtic Christian community

Philip Morris

For my wife, Sheila, with love and thanks
for all your support over the years.

First impression: 2020
Second impression: 2022

The publishers wish to acknowledge the support of
the Books Council of Wales

Cover photograph: Philip Morris
Cover design: Philip Morris & Y Lolfa

ISBN: 978 1 78461 753 0

Published and printed in Wales
on paper from well-maintained forests by
Y Lolfa Cyf., Talybont, Ceredigion SY24 5HE
website www.ylolfa.com
e-mail ylolfa@ylolfa.com
tel 01970 832 304
fax 832 782

Contents

FOREWORD

The Most Revd Barry Morgan
Archbishop of Wales 2003–2017

IT IS DIFFICULT to imagine now that Llanilltud Fawr was in the late fifth and early sixth centuries probably host to one of Britain's earliest centres of learning. It contained a school for young children and a training college for clergy and missionaries as well as being a monastery, all on one site, and was presided over by a man called Illtud, known for his love of the Scriptures and deep spirituality. It is also difficult to believe that a scholarly and critical in-depth study of such an important site has not been attempted before. This book by the Venerable Philip Morris – who has both lived and worked in the town as a priest and who was later to become the Archdeacon of Margam, with oversight of this area – has now plugged that gap splendidly. The modest subtitle 'The story of a Celtic Christian community' underplays the range of this book. It actually tells the story of this community from Neolithic and Iron Age times; its origins as a Christian community before Illtud's arrival; the community under Illtud and those who were his students; gives an account of what happened under the Vikings and then the Normans; goes on to recount the huge changes at the time of the Reformation; and brings the story right up to date with the present church and its restored Galilee Chapel, where important archaeological artefacts are displayed in an imaginative and magnificent way. This church, now in the centre of the town, is sited in a different place from the original monastic site made of wood, wattle and daub, which was probably nearer the coast on land possibly donated by King Meirchion in the late fifth century.

The strength of this book is that it does not claim too much, either for Illtud or the town named after him. The author has tried to extrapolate what might reasonably be said about the saint by a critical reading of the sources, especially the Life of Illtud written about him in the twelfth century, nearly six hundred years after his death. Like the writings about many saints, this is hagiographical in character: a fact overlooked by later writers about Illtud in the eighteenth and nineteenth centuries, who also adopted a romantic and uncritical view both of the early Saints and of Celtic Christianity in general. Instead Archdeacon Philip draws on the Life of Saint Samson, who with Gildas and Paul Aurelian is said to have studied under Illtud. This was written in the seventh century by a monk from Dol in Brittany, where Samson as bishop founded many churches – some of which he named after Illtud, although Illtud himself probably never visited Brittany. Since this was written nearer to the time when Illtud lived, it is more likely to reflect monastic and scholastic life at that time. Archdeacon Philip also draws on other historical and archaeological sources of the time, but again never uses them to claim too much.

However, he does correctly claim that the Christian faith was rooted in Wales before the coming of Saint Augustine to Kent in 597, but that too much has been claimed in the past about a separate Celtic church and spirituality in the early centuries. Instead he rightly, in my view, insists that there was a Romano-British church, owing allegiance to Rome, with its own emphases and culture but in an uneasy and ambivalent relationship with the Archbishop of Canterbury. This continued until the Normans divided England and Wales into territorial dioceses, with the four Welsh ones coming under Canterbury's jurisdiction. In a book of under 200 pages, Archdeacon Philip manages to convey the salient and essential points about the development of this community over its long history, and in so doing has put future historians in his debt.

INTRODUCTION

The parish
has a saint's name time cannot
unfrock.

These lines from the poet R.S. Thomas' 'The Moon in Lleyn'[1] could apply to Llantwit Major, where the name of its founder has been preserved in its Welsh form, Llanilltud Fawr, 'the great community of Illtud'. In the early twelfth-century Book of Llandaff, a compilation of earlier charters, it appears as Lannildut; but in charters of 1180 as Landiltwit; and in 1261 as Laniltwit. Rice Merrick barely mentions the place in his *A Booke of Glamorganshires Antiquities* (1578),[2] calling it Llan Iltuit. By the time the antiquarian Benjamin Heath Malkin visited in 1803, it was known as Llantwit Major.[3] But although time has preserved the memory of St Illtud in the town's Welsh name, many of its visitors – and indeed many of its residents – are unaware of his story. After all, Illtud is very much in the second division of saints, not featuring in the lists of the Catholic or Anglican Church except in Brittany and Wales. When he does, he is a shadowy figure, and any factual details of his life are overlaid with legend. The American website *Catholic Online* has this entry for St Illtud:

> One of the most revered saints of Wales, by tradition a cousin of the fabled King Arthur of the Britons. Reportedly a Briton, he and his wife Tyrnihild lived as members of a Glamorgan chief's army until they became hermits near the River Nadafan. Illtyd then studied with St Dubricius and founded the great abbey of Llanilltud Fawr in Glamorgan, Wales. He was a disciple of St Cadoc. According to one Welsh legend, Illtyd was one of the three Knights of the Holy Grail. He died in Brittany.[4]

9

As we will see, this is based on an untrustworthy twelfth-century *Vita Iltuti* (Life of St Illtud), but the Arthurian connection has been exploited down through the centuries, even to the extent of claiming King Arthur was Welsh as a result of Illtud's supposed kinship. The historical Illtud needs rescuing from the figure of legend.

The town of Llantwit Major lies just off the Glamorgan Heritage Coast, between Barry and Bridgend. The eighteenth-century bard Iolo Morganwg stated[5] that there were at least 2,000 pupils at the sixth-century monastic school. It seems likely that Iolo's figure is highly exaggerated, but if not, the town did not reach that level of population again until the 1950s. For many centuries, Llantwit Major was a small village in a prosperous agricultural area: the population in 1841 was 746, only rising by a hundred over the next 50 years. However, with the development of nearby RAF St Athan in the 1930s, local authority housing was built to the south of the town, and from the 1960s onwards considerable private housing. The result is that the population of Llantwit Major now stands at 14,500 and is rising, with a number of new housing developments under construction.

The property page of a national newspaper recently described Llantwit Major as a "snoozy, unassuming town",[6] and the Centre for Economic and Business Research in 2014 named the town as "the second most desirable place in Wales to live".[7] The old centre of Llantwit Major has always been confusing to visitors. Writing in 1938, C.J.O. Evans described it thus:

> Its picturesque, crooked streets, narrow and winding, are the nightmare of motorists, and its many exits are the despair of visitors, who often find themselves leaving the town by the wrong road.[8]

An old tradition for this "medieval maze" is that "the town is thus built the better to confound and confuse all enemies, pirates, smugglers and spies, who cannot escape once they are in our midst".[9]

An outer bypass was opened in 1978 and an inner one followed, which greatly eased traffic congestion in the old part of the town: the result is that it has the feel of an overgrown village. The Town Square, with the Town Hall (originally the Guildhall and Court House) and three pubs surrounding the War Memorial, is an interesting mixture of buildings dating from the sixteenth to the eighteenth centuries. Church Street leads down to St Illtud's Church, which is set low and accessed by a flight of steps, though the parallel Burial Lane allows a level entry.

The notion that Christianity came to this country with St Augustine in 597 was for long the traditional teaching: that the country was almost entirely pagan when Augustine landed in Britain. Even as late as 1997, the organisers of Pilgrims' Way, commemorating Augustine's arrival, took some persuading to bring an arm of the pilgrimage through south Wales, and particularly to Llantwit Major. In the event, they did so: on 2 June 1997, 500 people descended on the town. Many of those who had come from England commented that they had not been aware that there was a monastic school here a century prior to Augustine's mission, and for that reason it could be rightly called 'the cradle of Welsh Christianity'.

The great interest in 'Celtic Christian spirituality' that has developed over the last 30 years or so has helped to redress the balance and correct the perception that Britain was an entirely pagan land after the Romans left. However, it is to places such as Lindisfarne and Iona that the crowds flock: a whole industry has been developed around those islands that can sometimes detract from their spiritual impact. In Wales, Caldey Island is an attraction for day trippers from Tenby, though few realise that the modern Cistercian monastery maintains the tradition of a Celtic Christian foundation to which monks from Llanilltud made their retreat. Off the Llŷn Peninsula in north

Wales, Bardsey Island requires more of an effort to visit. It is now at the end of *Taith Pererin Gogledd Cymru*, the North Wales Pilgrims' Way. St David's Cathedral rightly has its fair share of visitors too – but so should Llanilltud, especially if there is any substance in the tradition that the patron saint of Wales studied there.

For over 400 years, the Galilee Chapel at the west end of St Illtud's Church in Llantwit Major was in a ruinous state. On 2 November 2013, the restored chapel was formally opened as "a place for visitors to experience, learn and be inspired by the amazing heritage, ongoing history, and living faith of this ancient holy site".[10] The Galilee Chapel displays the church's collection of early medieval stones: previously, in Simon Jenkins' words, these were "casually littering the western building, now filled with Sunday school clutter".[11] This has certainly enhanced the visitor experience, enabling the stones to be viewed from all sides and providing an opportunity to reflect on the Celtic Christian heritage of Llanilltud. Leaflets at the church say that "the story of Llanilltud is one of the greatest untold stories in Welsh history". This book is part of the process of telling that story and providing an understanding of the history and life of the Christian Church in Wales.

1

Llanilltud Before St Illtud

THE BARD IOLO MORGANWG (1747–1826) called the Vale of Glamorgan "Britain's Paradise" and the "Garden of Wales" as a testament to the beauty of this agricultural area, which has been farmed for millennia. There is evidence of human settlement along the Glamorgan Heritage Coast during the Neolithic Age, between 3500 BC and 2000 BC, with long barrows at Nash Point and Dunraven and the discovery of cultivated grasses at Ogmore-by-Sea, all within ten miles of Llantwit Major. During excavations for a new housing development at St Athan, a couple of miles east of Llantwit Major, a Neolithic enclosure was unearthed and pottery and flint were found. These are being analysed by the National Museum of Wales in Cardiff, and will provide important new evidence relating to the lives and deaths of people belonging to the early farming communities of the Vale of Glamorgan. During the Bronze Age (2000 BC to 750 BC) people moved back and forth across the Bristol Channel (which was much narrower than it is today) for trade and settlement. They perhaps used the estuary of the Afon Colhuw as a port, at what is now Llantwit Major. In 1940, Sir Cyril Fox excavated a turf barrow at Six Wells, just north of Llantwit Major, and found evidence of residential huts dating back to c.1000 BC.[12]

The earliest example of an Iron Age feasting site in Wales was discovered in 2003 at Llanmaes, adjoining Llantwit Major.

Cremated remains on the site have been dated to between about 2150 BC and 1950 BC. Objects found from the following period show that there must have been a settlement there until about 675 BC, which was subsequently abandoned and then used only for feasting. Thousands of pig bones, feasting vessels, bronze cauldrons, pottery and axes were unearthed, dated to from 600 BC to 10 BC, and also a large Iron Age enclosure. The cauldrons and axes were made in north-west France: this suggests that people came to Llanmaes for the feasting from the continent as well as Britain, again perhaps using the port at Llantwit Major.

The Celts

So who were these people who came to the Vale of Glamorgan – and other parts of Wales – from 600 BC onwards? They are commonly called the Celts, the name given in Greek *(Keltoi)* and Roman *(Celtae)* literature to the people of western continental Europe who were not Greek or Roman. However, for over a thousand years after the end of the Roman Empire in the fifth century, the term Celts was not used and it does not appear even in the Venerable Bede's *Ecclesiastical History of the English People* (731 AD). With the efforts of scholars of the seventeenth and eighteenth centuries trying to reconstruct prehistory, there arose the modern concept of a common Celtic language for those countries with a shared linguistic descent in France, Britain and Ireland, developed through an invasion of Celtic tribes from central Europe. However, although there are similarities between the later surviving Breton, Cornish, Welsh, Manx, Irish and Scots Gaelic languages, there have also developed considerable differences, to the extent that the people of one nation would not have generally understood people of another. Similarly, after the post-Roman and early medieval period, there is a popular misconception that there was a unified Celtic Christian Church with a common spirituality, which has been reconstructed into the modern 'Celtic worship' found in many Christian traditions today – a topic to which we will return later.

So we have from 600 BC onwards a movement of people across Europe, who for convenience we now call the Celts – on the basis of language – to distinguish them from the Romans or Greeks, assimilating with the native people of the places in which they settled. This was not an organised migration, as the Celts were fragmented, and did not all come from the same area; they came in clans, choosing an area for the clan to settle, to build their villages of timber or clay huts and farm the land. A reconstruction of an Iron Age homestead can be found at the National History Museum at St Fagans, near Cardiff.

The Celts were presented in classical literature as barbaric war-mongering warriors, as opposed to the civilised, cultured Romans. Propaganda through alternative facts and fake news was as prevalent then as it is alleged to be today. While it is true that the Celts had a fighting spirit, with wars between clans as much as against the Romans in order to control the best farming land, it is also true that the Celts were skilled in art, particularly metalwork, and in agriculture, developing the ox-drawn iron plough.

The Celtic or Iron Age villages were frequently set within extensive hill forts, defended by banks and ditches. There are three hill forts close to Llantwit Major, at Nash Point, Summerhouse Point and above Afon Colhuw. It has to be remembered that the Bristol Channel was narrower then than it is now: coastal erosion and the effect of storm surges have meant an estimated annual average cliff loss of 24 inches over the last 2,000 years at Colhuw. Assuming the outer defences of the hill forts were at the cliff edge, each one extended over three quarters of a mile more than at present, covering a large enough area to provide dwellings for the clan. While there has been limited archaeological exploration of the sites, fragments of pottery and hand mills that have been discovered there testify to the domestic use of the hill forts. It is to be hoped that

15

the Cherish Project of the Royal Commission on the Ancient and Historical Monuments of Wales, which is employing innovative techniques to discover, assess, map and monitor heritage coastal sites on land and beneath the sea, will help us understand more of the usage of these hill forts, as they are significant in determining the later siting of St Illtud's *llan* or monastic enclosure.

The Celtic clans in south-east Wales formed a loose confederation or tribe, named the Silures by Roman writers. Tacitus wrote:

> ...the swarthy faces of the Silures, the curly quality, in general, of their hair, and the position of Spain opposite their shores, attest to the passage of Iberians in old days and the occupation by them of these districts...[13]

This identification of the Celts of south-east Wales with the Iberian peninsula is significant in that recent research suggests that the Celtic language in its various forms did not originate from the peoples of Central Europe but from a branch of Indo-European in the western Mediterranean, then flowed north through Spain into the western Atlantic seaboard and the British Isles, later spreading back east into central Europe. Similarly, modern genetic studies have shown a genetic similarity between some of the Welsh and the Basques of Iberia, today's northern Spain and southern France.[14]

The Silures, through their network of hill forts, were extremely successful in waging guerrilla warfare against the Roman invaders from 47 AD until about 75 AD, even defeating a whole Roman legion. Despite their eventual military defeat, through assimilation of the invaders, the Silures' Brythonic language, art and culture lived on through the early medieval period. Their descendants would have been the people among whom St Illtud lived and worked, and who studied at his monastic school.

The Romans

The Roman invasion of Britain began in 48 AD but the conquest of south Wales was not completed until 78 AD. The occupation continued for three hundred years before the legions of soldiers were finally withdrawn.

Llantwit Major lies five miles south of the Roman road and the small military camp at Cowbridge. In 1888, excavations took place at Caermead Farm on the northern outskirts of Llantwit Major, at what had been identified as an extensive Roman villa, in occupation from the second to the fourth century AD.[15] Fifteen rooms were exposed, leading off a corridor. Some walls had stood to a height of nine feet and an aisled hall had a coloured mosaic floor, dated to the mid fourth century. Various agricultural buildings spread out from the main villa, suggesting that this was the home of a prosperous farmer, perhaps a Romanised Silurian.

The fact that there was a Roman villa at Llantwit Major illustrates the pattern of settlement during the later Roman period. Villas were built near the Roman military bases and towns such as Caerwent, Cardiff and Cowbridge, perhaps by retired soldiers or the indigenous inhabitants who were willing to accept the Roman occupation. In the case of the latter, they were allowed to farm their lands and follow their own local laws and customs. In this way the Brythonic language was preserved, though Latin words were assimilated into it and have survived in modern Welsh.

Excavations in 1948 at the Llantwit Major villa revealed four skeletons, thought to be of farm servants; the position and the crossing of the arms suggesting they were Christians. An excavation in 1971 and carbon dating of two of the skeletons showed one to have been from between 620 and 690 and the other from between 790 and 990. This has led to the conclusion that, following the villa's abandonment, the site was used as a burial place, perhaps by the community of Llanilltud.

It would have been exciting if the skeletons had been dated from before Illtud, but it is not too fanciful to conjecture that there were Christians in the area during the Roman period. Gildas, a pupil at Llanilltud, mentions the two Caerleon martyrs, Julius and Aaron, along with Alban, the first English martyr,[16] in his *De Excidio et Conquestu Britanniae* (On the Ruin and Conquest of Britain). The Venerable Bede, following Gildas, writes that, in the same persecution during which Alban was martyred, "...suffered Aaron and Julius, citizens of the City of Legions, and many others of both sexes throughout the land. After they had endured many horrible physical tortures, death brought an end to their struggles".[17] Julius and Aaron's martyrdom is traditionally thought to have taken place during the Diocletian persecution of Christians in 304. The Christian symbol of the Chi Rho has been found on a Roman pewter vessel at Caerwent (Venta Silurum) in Gwent, the capital of the Silures.

Following the Battle of the Milvian Bridge in 312, the victorious Emperor Constantine recognised Christianity as an imperial religion, thus ending the persecution of Christians and resulting in an expansion of the Church. The sea routes from the Mediterranean, the Iberian Peninsula and Brittany were significant in bringing merchants and traders to south Wales, and with them Christianity. Serving soldiers are known to have become Christians, along with other colonists, as well as native Celts. While there is little archaeological evidence and no documentation from the time, it is probable that the Christian faith spread throughout south Wales in the fourth and fifth centuries, particularly in the larger centres of population, though the old pagan religions were still prevalent. The Council of Nicaea in 325 had determined that capitals of provincial districts should have a bishop responsible for the oversight and pastoral care of the area. Whether or not the Church in south Wales was organised in any recognisable way in the fourth century is uncertain; while there is evidence of an organised Christian community at Caerwent meeting in houses, it is not known whether it was led by a bishop as it was later.

Post Roman

Roman legions were withdrawn from Wales in 383 by Magnus Maximus, the western Roman Emperor, so that they could be involved in his invasion of Gaul. Little is known of what happened in the immediate aftermath in south-east Wales, but we can assume that the native Silurians continued their agricultural way of life in this relatively prosperous area. However, soon things became anything but settled. Conflict grew between the various Brythonic Celtic kingdoms of Wales, the Anglo-Saxon kingdom of Mercia was trying to push westward and Irish raiders were attacking the south Wales coast and moving up the River Severn.

The earliest reliable reference to a bishop having episcopal oversight in south Wales is to be found in the *Vita Samsonis* (Life of St Samson). Writing in *c.*610, the author describes how *papa* (father) Dubricius (or Dyfrig in Welsh) came to Llanilltud to ordain Samson as deacon,[18] and later consecrated him bishop.[19] There are other references to Dubricius throughout the Life, variously according him the title 'Bishop' or 'Holy Father'. The probable date of Samson's consecration as bishop is 22 February 521,[20] suggesting that Dubricius had oversight of the area from the late fifth century onwards, probably from before the foundation of Illtud's monastic school; the *Liber Landavensis* (Book of Llandaff) says that it was Bishop Dubricius who appointed Illtud as abbot. The *Liber Landavensis* shows Dubricius as having his base in the territory of Ergyng, south-west Herefordshire, i.e. the *civitas* of Ariconium (later Archenfield), but this has more to do with the Diocese of Llandaff laying claim over that area than with historical fact. It is more likely that Dubricius' episcopal seat was at Caerwent, the former Roman capital of the Silures, his

19

authority extending as far west as Caldey Island and including Glamorgan.

The beginning of the sixth century was a turbulent period in Welsh history. The old kingdom of the Silurians was divided up into smaller territories: the greater part of south Wales formed the kingdom of Glywysing, perhaps with its capital at Dinas Powys, stretching from the River Usk to the River Loughor; much of this was by the tenth century to become Morgannwg or Glamorgan. Glywysing itself was divided into cantrefs, Gorfynydd forming the westernmost and stretching as far as the Gower Peninsula, with its *llys* or royal court at Llysworney, three miles north of Llanilltud.

We may infer that when Illtud arrived at that "most beautiful of places",[21] the valley of the River Hoddnant, there was already a Christian presence in this rich agricultural area. Although the Church had not yet been organised into dioceses, there was a bishop giving leadership and pastoral oversight. Christians met for worship in houses, though in some of the wealthier villas a separate building may have been constructed. There was considerable contact with the western seaboard of Europe, with ports along the Bristol Channel including Llantwit Major; and so there was an awareness of the wider Christian tradition, particularly of Brittany. The Romans had long left; despite the spread of Christianity, the old pagan religions remained, so the area was ripe for evangelism and needed a base for missionary activities.

Pelagianism

However, perhaps the more pressing need was for orthodox Christian teaching. The form of Christianity which had a strong following in Britain during the early fifth century was regarded by the Church in Rome as heretical, as the belief was spreading that original sin did not taint human nature and that mortal will was still capable of choosing good or evil without the need of God's grace other than as a means of instruction.

In other words, humans could earn salvation by their own efforts. This was Pelagianism, derived from the teaching of Pelagius, a British monk who lived from *c.*354 to *c.*420. One of his opponents, St Jerome (*c.*347–*c.*420), thought he was from Ireland, calling him "a porridge-sodden Irishman".[22] Another opponent was St Augustine of Hippo (354–430). According to Augustine, Pelagius spent "a very long time" in Rome writing a Commentary on the Epistles of St Paul, and then in Africa and Jerusalem. In 411 he was condemned at the Council of Carthage, and again at the Council of 418, after which he was expelled from Jerusalem. From there he fled to Egypt, where he died a few years later.

Following the Council of Carthage in 418, the Emperor Honorius decreed that all those who held the views of Pelagianism should be tried and sent into exile. Many Pelagians took refuge in Britain: according to Bede, they followed Agricola the son of Severianus, a Pelagian prelate, with the result that the heresy "seriously infected the faith of the British Church".[23] Bede tells us that being unable to refute Pelagianism's "plausible arguments by controversial methods", the British Church sought help from the bishops of Gaul. Meeting together in synod, the bishops chose Bishops Germanus of Auxerre and Lupus of Troyes to go to the Britons "to confirm their belief in God's grace". Germanus and Lupus' mission appeared to be successful and "the island of Britain was rapidly influenced by the reasoning, preaching, and virtues of these apostolic bishops [...] Catholics everywhere were strengthened and heretics corrected." Pelagians challenged the two, appearing with "rich ornaments and magnificent robes"; Bede helpfully explains that it was "on one side human presumption, on the other divine faith; on one side pride, on the other piety; on one side Pelagius, on the other Christ." Once the two felt that the heresy had been put down, they visited the tomb of St Alban, the first British martyr, at Verulamium in order to give thanks to God.

Then Bede relates the story of the 'Alleluia Victory'. The Saxons and the Picts were making war on the Britons, who called on the two bishops for help. During Lent, people came to the bishops for instruction in readiness for receiving the sacrament of Baptism on Holy Saturday night. "Strong in faith and fresh from the waters of baptism", the Britons were ready for battle. Germanus promised to direct the battle and set an ambush for the approaching enemy. "Suddenly Germanus, raising the standard, called upon them all to join him in a mighty shout. While the enemy advanced confidently, expecting to take the Britons unawares, the bishops three times shouted, 'Alleluia!' The whole army joined in this shout, until the surrounding hills echoed with the sound." The cries were so terrifying to the Saxons and the Picts that they fled or were drowned in the river, and the British won the battle without striking a blow.[24]

The 'Alleluia Victory' has been dated to 429. Bede had obviously read a biography of Germanus written by Constantius of Lyon about forty years after the mission to Britain; indeed he copied phrases verbatim. While some scholars dispute some of the details in Constantius' account of Germanus and Lupus' mission, it does show the seriousness in which the Pelagian heresy was held and the impact of Germanus and Lupus' preaching. However, soon after their return to Gaul, Germanus had to return to Britain as the Pelagian heresy was being promulgated again. Constantius and Bede tell how, as the result of Germanus healing the son of Elafius, one of the leading men of the country, the Catholic faith was firmly implanted in the hearts of all people; the false teachers were banished to the Continent, and "henceforward, the Faith was maintained uncorrupted in Britain for a long time".[25]

But how long was 'a long time'? More than a century after Germanus' second visit, a synod had to be held at Llanddewi Brefi in Ceredigion, according to Rhygyfarch's *Vita Sancti David* (Life of St David), as "the Pelagian heresy was reviving, introducing the vigour of its stubbornness, like the venom of a poisonous serpent, into the inmost joints of the country".[26] As a result of David's preaching, aided by a hill rising up under his feet so that the crowds could hear him, "the heresy is expelled. The faith is confirmed in sound hearts. All are in agreement. They pay thanks to God and to Saint David."[27]

The fact that Pelagianism was never far below the surface in fifth- and sixth-century Britain meant that people needed to be schooled in orthodox Christian teaching and trained to preach and teach the faith – and this is exactly what a monastic school such as Llanilltud could provide. Although Llanilltud is credited by the *Guinness Book of Records* as Britain's earliest centre of learning, it is possible that a number were set up as a result of Germanus' teaching. The *Vita Samsonis* mentions a tradition that the monastery at Llanilltud "had been founded by St Germanus"[28] and calls Illtud "a disciple of St Germanus".[29] The further claim that Germanus had ordained Illtud priest is obviously historically inaccurate, but does indicate that Illtud was following the teaching and tradition of Germanus. Is it possible that a monastic school was already in existence at Llanilltud before Illtud's arrival?

The Rise of Monasticism

It is difficult to be certain when the concept of men or women living together in a Christian community came to Britain. Bede implies an early date for St Ninian's monastery at Whithorn, Dumfries and Galloway, south-west Scotland, on the basis that Ninian named its church after St Martin of Tours, who had established the first monastery in the west in about 350. A later Life of St Ninian tells how he visited Tours following a period of study in Rome, and was so impressed by Martin living the life of a monk that he decided to build a similar monastery in Galloway. Ninian was born in 360; Martin died in 397, so Ninian's visit must have been sometime before then. While of course any date is subject to conjecture, it would seem that

Whithorn is the earliest monastic foundation in Scotland, supporting its claim to be the cradle of Scottish Christianity. It later had a monastic school as well as a church built of stone, and was known as *Candida Casa*, the White House.

St Martin had been a soldier in the Roman army, towards the end of his career changing his allegiance from the emperor Caesar Julian to Christ as his new commanding officer. Settling at Tours in France, he was ordained and reluctantly became Bishop of Tours, later withdrawing to become a monk. The story of Martin changing from soldier to monk may have influenced the twelfth-century writer of the *Vita Iltuti*, who tells of Illtud similarly changing career, giving rise to the tradition of *Illtud Farchog*, Illtud the knight.

The ascetic tradition of monasticism as withdrawing from the world can be traced back to at least the third century. The foundation of Christian monasticism is credited to Anthony of Egypt (252–356), who lived as a hermit in the desert, but gained followers who lived as hermits nearby though not in actual community with him. By the fourth century, more organised communities were developing in Egypt, with monks living in individual huts or cells but worshipping, eating and working together, following a monastic Rule by which they lived their lives. St John Cassian (*c*.360–*c*.435), a friend of St Germanus, with whom he had experienced monastic life in Palestine and Egypt, founded a community of monks and another of nuns near Marseilles. In his two long works, the *Institutes* and *Conferences*, he set out the ideals of monasticism, establishing its theological and evangelical basis.

Germanus no doubt taught the ideals of monasticism as set out by his friend John Cassian, seeing it as a way of combating Pelagianism. Although there is no direct evidence, it is possible that monastic communities were founded in Britain as a result, including perhaps one at Llanilltud. It has been suggested that Germanus used the western approaches to Britain on his second mission,[30] and therefore could have visited south Wales.

We do not know how far Ninian's influence spread south from Whithorn, but he too was involved in challenging the Pelagian heresy. There were significant connections and considerable travel between communities in the west of Britain through the sea routes of the Irish Sea and contact with Gaul, Spain and North Africa. Imported pottery from the east Mediterranean and Egypt has been found at the Iron Age fort at the possible capital of the kingdom of Glywysing at Dinas Powys, east of Llantwit Major, some dated to the fifth century and some earlier than 400.[31] Not only would merchants use the sea routes through the Mediterranean to south Wales, but also pilgrims to and from the Holy Land and Christians from North Africa, all spreading information about the monastic way of life in that area.

Gerald of Wales, in his *Descriptio Kambriae* (The Description of Wales), written soon after 1188, attributed some of the spiritual practices of the Welsh that he observed in his day to Germanus and Lupus: for example giving bread to the poor, tithing, showing respect to monks and priests, and reverence towards relics of the saints, bells, holy books and the Cross.[32] Gerald's observation was that "...this is the reason why the churches in Wales are more quiet and tranquil than those elsewhere".

There is no documentary evidence of an early connection between the Church in south Wales and the Church in Ireland, but there is a tradition that St Patrick was born in Wales in the early fifth century: the British town of Bannaventa Berniae that Patrick mentions in his *Confessions* as his birthplace has not been identified, but a very local tradition claims that it is Banwen in the Dulais Valley north of Neath. In his *Confessions*, Patrick says that he was captured when about sixteen years of age and taken from his home to Ireland. After some years, having escaped before being recaptured and escaping again, he returned to his family in Britain to study Christianity. Muirchú's *Vita Sancti Patricii* (Life of St Patrick) says that he made a journey across Gaul, discovering Germanus at Auxerre and being taught "knowledge, wisdom, chastity and everything useful for mind and soul".[33] Patrick was obviously influenced by the ideals of monastic life, and on returning to Ireland as a missionary he encouraged men and women to take monastic vows: "The sons of the Irish and daughters of kings are even becoming monks and virgins of Christ."[34] We do not how monasticism was organised in Ireland during the fifth century: Patrick is silent on that.

Monasticism was seen in the late fifth and early sixth century as the Christian ideal, the life to which every Christian should aspire; through the influence of such people as Ninian, Germanus and Patrick, it was beginning to be practised in Britain and Ireland. While there was not the kind of monastic organisation or structure that is found in the later medieval period, for example among the Benedictines and Cistercians, it would seem that small communities began to spring up in many parts of the country. Although there is no documentary or archaeological evidence for these, by the early sixth century larger monasteries had been well established throughout the country, such as at Llanilltud and Llancarfan; and by the time Gildas, trained at Llanilltud, wrote *De Excidio et Conquestu Britanniae*, his history of the British people, in 540, there were factions within the monastic movement. All of this suggests there was a gestation period in the late fifth century. This allows us to surmise that small Christian communities may have already been in existence at places such as Llanilltud before the arrival of Illtud and Llancarfan before the arrival of Cadoc, following the axiom that 'absence of evidence does not provide evidence of absence'.

2

The Life of St Illtud

Sources for the Life of St Illtud

No pre-Norman Life of St Illtud remains; the earliest is the *Vita Iltuti*,[35] which appears to have been written early in the twelfth century by one of the *clerus Sancti Iltuti*, the 'clergy of St Illtud'. He writes in the past tense about William Rufus, the son of William the Conqueror, and Robert Fitzhamon, the Norman ruler of Glamorgan; Robert died in 1107, so the *Vita Iltuti* must have been written sometime after that date.

The writer of the twelfth-century *Vita Iltuti* describes the setting of Llanilltud as "the most beautiful of places". A wide, flat valley through which flows a river, woods on either side, the sea in close proximity, which would at times flood the valley, the clifftop fort: we see the same topography today. However, there is very little in the *Vita Iltuti* that can be treated as historical fact, being overlaid by miraculous happenings, dubious royal connections, and unsavoury dealings with Illtud's wife.

The *Vita Iltuti* was written at a critical time in Welsh Church history, when the pre-Norman *clasau* or communities were being brought within the jurisdiction of the bishop of each of the newly created territorial dioceses. Lives of the early founders of the communities were sometimes written to show the claim of the diocese over the *clas* and its lands by exaggerating an ancient connection; sometimes they were written to show the importance of one *clas* over another. It was a case of reconstructing the past to justify the present or prepare for the future. So in the *Vita Iltuti*, we are told that Illtud went to Dubricius (Dyfrig) "the Bishop of Llandaff" to receive his clerical habit and tonsure, and "the Bishop Dubricius" came to the Hoddnant Valley, "marking out the boundary of a cemetery, and in the midst, in honour of the supreme and undivided Trinity, the foundation of an oratory". In the introduction to the *Liber Landavensis* (Book of Llandaff), which is a book of charters and saints' lives contemporary with the *Vita Iltuti*, its compiler says that Dubricius appointed Illtud as abbot of the monastery "called after him Lannildut" as part of his organisation of the diocese of Llandaff. The historical inaccuracy – as dioceses were not organised in this way in the sixth century – is to justify the fact that by the early twelfth century the community at Llanilltud was under the oversight of the Bishop of Llandaff.

The *Vita Iltuti* follows the usual formula for the twelfth-century Lives of the saints: Illtud's birth and early life, his education, his establishing of the monastery of Llanilltud, various miracles, Illtud's life as a hermit, and his death. In addition there are two chapters describing events that must have happened within very recent memory; it is the final chapter that mentions William Rufus and Robert Fitzhamon.

Although the *Vita Iltuti* is the only complete life – albeit not historical – of Illtud that survives, he is mentioned in a number of Lives of other saints that predate it. In the *Vita Cadoci* (Life of St Cadoc), written at the end of the eleventh century by Lifris, Archdeacon of Glamorgan and master of the monastery of Llancarfan, Illtud is given his monastic habit and tonsure not by Bishop Dubricius but by Cadoc, the Abbot of Llancarfan. Any attempt at historical accuracy is overtaken by the desire to show the primacy of the monastery of Llancarfan over its nearby rival, Llanilltud.

One would imagine that the closer in time to a saint that a mention is made of him or her in a manuscript, the more accurate it would be. However, there can still be confusion in detail, an emphasis on miracles, and a particular agenda that distorts facts. Towards the end of the ninth century, Wrmonoc, a native of Léon in Brittany, wrote the *Vita Pauli Aureliani* (Life of St Paul Aurelian) about the founder of Saint-Pol-de-Léon. Wrmonoc had not visited Llanilltud and confuses Illtud's school with Samson's monastery at Caldey. However, Wrmonoc describes Illtud as "a man of noble birth and great learning" and as having many disciples, including Paul Aurelian. Some of the miracles in the *Vita Pauli Aureliani* appear in the later *Vita Iltuti*, though the *Vita Pauli Aureliani* was not known in Wales at the time. Does this mean that there was an earlier Life of St Illtud in existence, adapted by Wrmonoc and the writer of the *Vita Iltuti* to suit their purposes?

There is a Life that gives us the earliest detailed information about Illtud and his *llan*, the *Vita Samsonis* (Life of St Samson),[36] which, from the use of particular geographical names, would appear to have been written at Dol in Brittany in about the year 610 – though some scholars claim a later date.[37] However, there is little of what is found in the *Vita Pauli Aureliani* and the *Vita Iltuti* in the earlier *Vita Samsonis*: the only common statements are that Illtud was a teacher and that Samson was one of his students. The writer tells us that St Samson (*c*.485–*c*.565) was brought by his parents "to the school of the famous master of the Britons, Eltut[38] by name"; was ordained deacon at Llanilltud by 'Papa' Dubricius; left soon after for Caldey Island; and returned later to be Abbot of Llanilltud, being ordained bishop. The *Vita Samsonis* provides us with a fascinating insight into life at Llanilltud in its early years, and particularly its liturgy.

The writer, who was a Breton monk, tells us that he was asked by a Cornish bishop, Tigernomalus, to write an account of the life of St Samson, although he felt "unworthy of and unfitted for the work". However, he commits himself to the task, and states, "I wish it to be believed that these words are not put together on the lines of rash surmising of my own, or of those of confused and unauthorised rumours; but on what I derived from a certain religious and venerable old man whose house beyond the sea Samson himself had founded." The old man in turn had heard about Samson from his nephew, Henoc, who was also Samson's cousin, with some of the details of his early life coming from Samson's mother. The writer of *Vita Samsonis* had visited Llanilltud: describing St Illtud, he says, "In his splendid monastery I have been." He had also been to Caldey, saying, "In this island I too have been." No doubt he heard more stories about Illtud and Samson from the monks in those two places.

Using these texts, with the caution that none provide us with a precise biography, and certainly with little historical accuracy, we can attempt to construct the life of St Illtud.

The life of St Illtud

It is to the early seventh-century *Vita Samsonis* that we must turn in order to try to discover something of the life of St Illtud, but even with that early manuscript we run into historical difficulties. The *Vita Samsonis* states: "Eltut was a disciple of St Germanus, and St Germanus himself had ordained him priest in his youth."[39] As Thomas Taylor says in a footnote in his translation of the *Vita Samsonis*, "If St Germanus died in 448 and Eltut was born in 436, this must be a mistake."[40] We have seen why the writer should link Illtud with Germanus, but what of Taylor's assertion that Illtud was born in 436?

The *Vita Samsonis* provides us with the strongest clues for dating Illtud, by computing the dates of St Samson's life. The *Vita Samsonis* tells us that Samson was ordained bishop on "the day of the blessed Apostle Peter's Chair (22 February)", which fell on a Sunday at the beginning of Lent.[41] From this, Taylor believes the probable year of Samson's consecration is 521;

assuming Samson was then 35, the canonical age for a bishop, he would have been born in 486.[42] The *Vita Samsonis* says that when Samson was about five years old, his parents brought him to "the school of the famous master of the Britons, Eltut by name".[43] This suggests that Illtud's monastic school was well established by 490. The *Vita Samsonis* does not mention Illtud in the appointment of Samson as Abbot of Llanilltud, or at his consecration as bishop, so Illtud had either retired or died by 521. So a date of 436 for Illtud's birth is not unreasonable.

What more does the *Vita Samsonis* tell us about Illtud?

In truth, Eltut was of all the Britons the most accomplished in all the Scriptures, namely of the Old and New Testaments, and in those of philosophy of every kind, of geometry namely, and of rhetoric, grammar and arithmetic, and of all the theories of philosophy. And by birth he was a most wise magician, having knowledge of the future.[44]

The writer is hesitant to say more about Illtud's "wonderful deeds" in case he be "led too far from our original undertaking": to write the Life of St Samson. However, he does go on to describe Illtud's death, but says that he does so "in order to establish our point" of Illtud having the gift of prophecy.

The story of Illtud's death was obviously remembered and became part of the oral tradition of the community at Llanilltud, certainly established enough ninety years later to be related to the writer of the *Vita Samsonis* in great detail. We are told that Illtud "was weighed down by mortal sickness of body"[45] and called two other 'abbats', Isanus and Atoclius, to visit him, greeting them with these words:

I rejoice, dearest brothers, at your arrival, forasmuch as the time of my departure and of my sleep in Christ is at hand, and you offer me deep respect... I indeed shall be taken by the hands of angels this night in your presence when it is hardly midnight; and on such wise that my brother Isanus will see my soul in the likeness of an eagle having two golden wings.

31

Illtud talked with Isanus and Atoclius "during a day and a night [...] calling much to mind".

> When it was nearly midnight, as he bade farewell to the brothers, he departed happily from this habitation of flesh amid hymns and choruses and the accustomed solemnities. And blessed Isanus saw his soul under the seeming likeness which he himself had mentioned...

The *Vita Samsonis* shows an educated and cultured man who has studied the Christian Scriptures, was ordained priest, was *magister* (master or teacher) and abbot of a monastic school, and who was revered by his successors. That is all: there is no indication of where Illtud came from, or his background and training once we dismiss the reference to Germanus, other than that Illtud was following in his tradition. The *Vita Samsonis* does, however, give us some interesting insights into life at the monastic school, which we will return to later.

The writer of the *Vita Samsonis* gave Eltut (Illtud) the title of Saint, as with Samson. While of course St Paul in his epistles gave the title Saint to the Christian faithful, within the Roman Catholic Church today there is a lengthy process before canonisation, which requires a person to have lived a life of 'heroic virtue' and to have had verified miracles attributed to prayers made to the individual after their death to prove that they are in heaven. But within the first thousand years or so of the Christian Church there was no such process, and local tradition would give a holy person the title Saint. Within Wales there are many dedications of churches to a saint about whom little or nothing is known, except perhaps for some local traditions. Illtud had a wider veneration than within Llanilltud; and as we will see, his influence can be traced through dedications of churches to him in Wales and Brittany.

From what is a fairly factual description of Illtud and of the monastic school by a writer diligent in his research, we move to the more fanciful writings with very little historical foundation. These were produced as propaganda to strengthen the interest of Llanilltud, whether it be over its rival, St Cadoc's monastery at Llancarfan, or the Norman diocese of Llandaff. It is unfortunate that some modern writers have constructed biographies of Illtud based on these writings and have thus promoted perceptions of him that are not based on fact. Sabine Baring-Gould and John Fisher use the twelfth-century *Vita Iltuti* as their primary source in their magisterial *Lives of the British Saints*,[46] detailing Illtud's connection to King Arthur, his life as a soldier, and the dismissal of his wife, none of which have any historical basis. A group of writers have used the supposed connection of Illtud with King Arthur to 'prove' that the king was really Welsh and that Illtud buried the monarch, taking his body up the River Ewenny to a cave near Pencoed; according to their theory, it was later placed in a crypt under the church of Peterston-super-Montem.[47] Chris Barber in *King Arthur: the Mystery Unravelled*, again to 'prove' that he was Welsh, claims that King Arthur, under the name of Arthmael, was born at Boverton in Llantwit Major, was a pupil at Llanilltud on the basis that rulers sent their sons to be taught there, and that he is commemorated on the Samson Cross, now displayed in the Galilee Chapel of St Illtud's Church in Llantwit Major.[48] In the same way that the early medieval Lives were written for a particular purpose, so it is with some of the modern writings in which reference is made to Illtud – even to promote tourism in Wales.

Although some writers, both past and present, have made much of Illtud's royal connection, there is actually only a passing reference in the *Vita Iltuti*: "the magnificent soldier (Illtud) hearing of the magnificence of his cousin, King Arthur, desired to visit the court of so great a conqueror".[49] The writer states that Illtud was born in Brittany to a Breton soldier called Bicanus and his wife Rieingulid, daughter of Anblaud, King of Britannia – a very suitable pedigree to bolster the twelfth-century claims of Llanilltud.[50] From post-Roman times there was a strong connection between Brittany and south Wales. This was romanticised in twelfth-century writings such as those of Geoffrey of Monmouth, who also popularised the Arthurian legends, so it is not surprising that the writer of *Vita Iltuti* should wish to show Illtud to be a Breton of some considerable standing.

The *Vita Iltuti* tells us that his parents, "in baptising the boy and after the washing of regeneration", named him "Iltutus, Illtud, to wit, *ille*, he, who is *tutus*, safe, from every fault", although this is a false etymology. Illtud's "parents vowed to dedicate him to literature, and they dedicate him so vowed to be instructed in the seven arts". Illtud "was a man of such memory that once hearing an instruction of his master, he retained it in his heart ever after." We are not told where or by whom Illtud was taught, but the writer was concerned to show the breadth of Illtud's knowledge, reflected in the subjects taught in his monastic school. However, "after instruction and after the knowledge taught was known to him, he laid aside the study of literature, applying himself to military training." Although we are not told where Illtud received this training either, the subsequent mention of King Arthur has given rise to later legends that this was at his court and that Illtud was one of the Knights of the Round Table. Illtud then went as a soldier, along with his wife Trynihid, to the court of Poulentus, "king of the Glamorgan folk" where, we are told, he presided over the royal household.[51] The tradition of *Illtud Farchog* – Illtud the knight – is very strong in Welsh literature and is found in the writings of bards such as Tudur Penllyn of north Wales (*c.*1420–*c.*1485–90) and Llywelyn ap Rhisiart of south Wales (1520–1565). Iolo Morganwg (1747–1826) described Illtud as "the studious golden-chained knight".

The earliest reference to Illtud's military background comes in the *Vita Cadoci*, written in about 1086 by Lifris, who is described in the *Liber Landavensis* as Archdeacon of Glamorgan and "master of Saint Catoc of Llanncarvan". St

Cadoc's monastic community at Llancarfan had by the eleventh century eclipsed Llanilltud; Lifris was concerned to preserve its premier position in the face of the determination of the Norman lords to subsume the former Celtic Christian communities into the new monastic foundations such as St Peter's Abbey in Gloucester and Robert Fitzhamon's St Mary's Abbey in Tewkesbury. Although Cadoc was not born until the late fifth century, Lifris makes him older than Illtud and responsible for his conversion from soldier to monk. He tells how fifty soldiers of a local chieftain, Pawl of Penychen, interrupted Cadoc while he was teaching the people, demanding food, which they threatened to take by force if he refused. Cadoc gave them loaves, a pig and beer, but the soldiers did not start eating until the arrival of their captain, Illtud, who had not been with them when they came to the monastery. On Illtud's arrival there was an earthquake, and the soldiers fell into a deep abyss. However, Illtud and the food and drink survived. Illtud rushed to Cadoc and "besought the man of God, with earnest entreaties, in the name of the divine majesty, that he would grant to him the monastic habit, and would intimate the same by giving him the marks of service, as the shaving of his hair and beard".[52] From then on, Illtud "changed his warfare for obtaining the highest crown." The food and drink were given to the poor.

There is no historical basis for Lifris' story, but it suited his purpose by making Llancarfan superior to Llanilltud and also by showing the Normans that there was a higher calling than that of a soldier. The later *Vita Iltuti* repeats the story, but with subtle differences: following the swallowing up of the soldiers into the ground, Illtud asked Cadoc for advice. Cadoc "advised him first to set aside the secular habit, then to seek again the clerical habit which he had discarded, and to serve the supreme Creator for the rest of his life for the sake of eternal repayment".[53] The writer tells us that Illtud asked the King for permission to leave his service, and "having received permission, withdrew himself from secular service". He says

Illtud took his wife and "armour bearers", arriving first at the River Nadauan; and then, having dismissed his wife, that he was made a monk at the Valley of Hoddnant by "Dubricius, Bishop of Llandaff." So Illtud returned to the life of study and prayer that he had led as a child.

In his account of Illtud's 'conversion', the twelfth-century writer of the *Vita Iltuti* has introduced an element which many, not treating it as unhistorical, find disturbing: the rejection by Illtud of his wife, Trynihid. We are told that an angel admonished Illtud in a dream, stressing that having a wife is a barrier if he is to be true to his vocation. "Love of wife also possesses thee that thou turnest not to the Lord. What, pray, is carnal love but a horror and the source of sins? [...] Thy wife is comely, but better is chastity." In the morning, when Trynihid came to Illtud, he "drove her off so wishing as the poison of a serpent, declaring he was leaving her, and saying 'Thou shalt not cling to me further.'"[54] Trynihid, after much pleading, eventually left and then devoted her single life to prayer and good works in the mountains, building a dwelling and an oratory. "She prayed constantly, being found blameless and irreprehensible in all her manner of life, remaining a nun, comforting innumerable widows and nuns and poor people in her charge."[55]

Unwisely, however, Trynihid decided to visit Illtud at Llanilltud. She did not recognise "the industrious digger, of muddy countenance owing to his constant delving; leanness too had attenuated the contours of his countenance." This was Illtud, "clothed as he was with goat's hair and skins, not as she had seen him formerly, a handsome soldier". Illtud refused to engage in conversation with her, and as a punishment for visiting him, Trynihid lost her sight. Illtud "implored the Lord's compassion that she might recover her former vision. His prayers being heard by God, she saw clearly; afterwards she returned corrected [...] Nevertheless, her countenance was not afterwards so fair as before, affected with spots and pallor

[...] as though ill with fever. Therefore she remained in the aforesaid place, never again visiting Saint Illtud because she was unwilling to displease God and the most beloved of God." Why should the writer of the *Vita Iltuti* invent such a story? As we have seen, the medieval Lives of earlier saints were written with a political aim: to demonstrate to the new Norman secular and ecclesiastical rulers that the pre-Norman monastic communities and their founders had credibility within the new order. From the fifth to the eleventh century, most clergy were married, especially in the western parts of Europe. St Germanus, who led the fight against Pelagianism and in whose tradition Illtud followed, was married to Eustachia, according to his biographer Constantius. Some of the later biographers were sons of clergy: Lifris, the writer of the *Vita Cadoci*, was the son of Herewald, who was Bishop of Llandaff from 1056 to 1104; and Rhygyfarch, who wrote the *Vita Sancti David*, was the eldest of the four sons of Bishop Sulien of St Davids. However, in synods in the early part of the twelfth century leading up to the Lateran Councils of 1123 and 1139, clergy marriages were declared unlawful and those married could not be ordained deacon, priest or bishop. From that time onwards, strict celibacy became the law of the Catholic Church.

The issue of clerical celibacy began to emerge during the fourth century with the growth of monasticism, which was seen as the ideal of the Christian life and implied celibacy. However, while ecclesiastical law books may have praised celibacy in the context of monasticism, it is not mentioned as far as clergy are concerned, and their marriage law does not exclude clerics. In actual fact, an early eighth-century Irish law book, the *Collectio canonum hibernensis* (Irish collection of canon law), assumes that clerics marry. Indeed, St Patrick was descended from priests and his father was a deacon, and bishops, priests and deacons are recorded as being married in the annals of the Irish Church. Similarly, the Irish monasteries were often comprised of communities of men and women living

37

together as families. There was a right of hereditary succession for the abbot of a monastery: Gerald of Wales (*c*.1146–*c*.1223) comments that sons of abbots would succeed to the position by hereditary right after the death of their fathers. If the abbot was not married or had no son, then the appointment would be of someone who was of the tribe of the founder of the community.

So the twelfth-century writer of the *Vita Iltuti* was presented with a problem. How could he show that Illtud had credibility as a married man when the ruling at the time was that clerical marriages were unlawful? Quite simply, by making Illtud send his wife away once he became a monk. The writer emphasised Illtud's celibacy on becoming a monk by showing how he resisted temptation when his wife pleaded that she might lie beside him in bed. The celibate Abbot Illtud thus has credibility amongst the twelfth-century ecclesiastical establishment, but also amongst the Norman lords, because this would help them in their quest to break up the clerical dynasties noted by Gerald of Wales. Illtud could very well have been married, but there is no reason for us to think that he would have sent his wife away in such a brutal manner – it is more likely that Llanilltud was a mixed community including husbands and wives and children within the monastic school.

Many of the written Lives of the saints are overladen with stories of miraculous happenings, intended to enhance the saint in question's reputation. Such stories present difficulties to the twenty-first-century mindset, but of course would not have done so in earlier times because they were seen as proof of sainthood. We do not have to accept them as historical fact, but accept the purpose for which the writers included them. While there is only one extant Life of St Illtud – and that written 600 years after his death – and there is limited mention of him in the Lives of other saints written earlier, we would expect stories to have been told about Illtud down through the centuries and to have been embellished as time went on.

However, in the seventh-century *Vita Samsonis*, miracles are attributed to Samson, but none to Illtud. In the ninth-century *Vita Pauli Aureliani* there is one miracle: St Paul Aurelian, St David, St Samson and St Gildas – pupils at Llanilltud – are said to have joined with Illtud in driving back the sea.[56] Llanilltud is described as being of a very limited area and hemmed in by the sea; the four pupils asked Illtud to pray to the Lord that he might "cause the sea to retire" so that the monastery could be enlarged. Illtud agreed, and the five prayed. Then Illtud and his pupils went down to the shore at low tide "when the sea used to withdraw to the distance of a mile or more";[57] Illtud traced a furrow with the point of his staff "beyond which he forbade the water to pass, and it has never since that time transgressed his command." Illtud attributed the miracle to his pupils; they ascribed it to him.

The story of the driving back of the sea is repeated at greater length in the twelfth-century *Vita Iltuti*, with no mention of Paul, David, Samson and Gildas, even though the writer has listed them earlier. It is a story that would no doubt have been repeated many times over the centuries and, as it grew, it was to Illtud alone that the miracle became attributed, showing how his community was able to have "marshy land having become dry" and fertile for agriculture, "and what was not arable, the clergy had in meadow and fodder abundance for cattle".[58] The particular value of this story today is in determining the original site of Llanilltud, as we shall see.

The driving back of the sea is one of surprisingly very few miracles as such recorded in the *Vita Iltuti*. The writer tells of Illtud having to hide in a cave as the result of persecution by King Meirchion, and being sent "from heaven" every ninth hour one loaf of barley bread, and one portion of fish.[59] Enemies are swallowed up by the earth or turned into stone, but this is not directly attributed to Illtud. However, in what was intended to be the final chapter of the *Vita Iltuti*, there is an account of a pilgrimage Illtud made to Mont-Saint-Michel, which the writer places in Brittany. This is obviously unhistorical, as Mont-Saint-Michel did not exist as a church and community until the eighth century. Before leaving, Illtud gave orders that the corn stored in three of Llanilltud's barns should, after threshing, be laid up in granaries until he returned. Illtud made the pilgrimage, but as he was about to embark on the return journey, he noticed that there was a severe famine and the people of Brittany were on the point of starvation.

> He was afflicted at the sight of such need as this; he felt for them, he besought the heavenly Helper to render help. His prayers being heard in the heavenly hall, the aforementioned corn was conveyed from on high, as he had wished it in his prayers to be carried, and was afterwards found in a harbour of Llydaw on the shore, whence the whole of Llydaw (that is, Britannia Minor, Brittany) fed itself, and moreover, sowed its cultivated lands. They magnify and render thanks to their helper, by whose prayers they had been defended from dangerous famine.[60]

The writer then tells how Illtud sailed back to Llanilltud, only to return to Brittany:

> ...and there at the monastery of Dol, his days being determined for him beforehand by his own Creditor, who has fixed for mortals the limits, which they will not be able to pass, his virtues and sanctity being accomplished, renowned for his miracles and celebrated for his signs and wonders, commending his body to the ground and his spirit of a truth to the Lord, departing from this mournful life on the eighth day before the Ides of November,[61] and being born to a lasting and celestial existence, and rejoicing to be about to live for ever, he passed over to the Lord, to whom is honour, power, and dominion for ever and ever, Amen.[62]

Placing Illtud's death at Dol is in contradiction of the writer of the *Vita Samsonis*, who was told "by our catholic brothers who dwelt in that place" that it was at Llanilltud.[63]

In reality, if we are looking for historical facts about St Illtud, we are going to be disappointed beyond what we can say with some certainty: that he was a fifth–sixth-century monk who was the master and abbot of a monastic school at a place we now call Llanilltud Fawr (Llantwit Major). The information about Illtud contained in the Lives of various saints from the seventh century onwards is contradictory; there would have been a certain amount of oral tradition handed down, and indeed some could have been contained in written manuscripts now lost. The most complete Life is too late and too political to be of any real use in reconstructing the historical Illtud, but we do have to recognise the purpose of one of the twelfth-century *clerus Sancti Iltuti* in writing it. No doubt chapters from the *Vita Iltuti* would have been read in the new collegiate church that replaced the pre-Norman monastery, particularly on St Illtud's festival day of 6 November as an encouragement to the clergy as they were going through a period of tremendous change, perhaps even having been relocated from their previous *llan* to the present site and certainly now coming under the control of the Benedictine Abbey of Tewkesbury. For 600 years, St Illtud had been revered as a holy and wise teacher, and the twelfth-century writer was determined that he should be so regarded for centuries to come.

3

Llanilltud in the Sixth Century

Introduction

The modern interest in Celtic Christianity arose in the last quarter of the twentieth century, with the appearance of an abundance of books showing that the pre-Norman period, commonly called the Dark Ages, was anything but dark, as the light of the Gospel shone brightly in Britain through saints such as Ninian, David, Columba and Aidan and their monastic foundations at Whithorn, Menevia, Iona and Lindisfarne.

One effect of the current popularity of all things Celtic is to see the pre-Norman Church in the countries now referred to as Celtic as being separate and isolated from the continental Church, and particularly from Rome, so that it was pure, free from the institutionalised organisation of the Catholic Church, and therefore able to focus on mission and evangelism. The phrase 'the Celtic Church' is used almost as if it were a denomination, encompassing the Church in Brittany, Cornwall, Wales, Scotland and Ireland. However, the Church in the Celtic lands cannot be seen in denominational terms, nor as a unified entity. Although those countries which we call Celtic are linked by a common linguistic background, each had – and still has - its own language and culture which would have made a common Church impossible despite the obvious interaction between them. Bede did not use the term 'Celtic' in his *Ecclesiastical History* and nor did any other writer in the pre-Norman period; modern academics prefer to talk about a Welsh Church in Wales, and similarly for the other Celtic countries. However it is convenient to use the linguistic term 'Celtic' when referring to those countries on the western fringes of northwest Europe and hence its use in the title of many academic books on the subject of Christianity in the Celtic lands without presupposing a common 'Celtic Church'. Some use the term 'early middle ages' or 'early medieval' for the pre-Norman period to avoid the use of the word 'Celtic'.

So if there was not a common 'Celtic Church', what was the relationship of the Welsh Church in Wales – and particularly the Church in south Wales – with the Catholic Church centred on Rome?

As we have seen, the variety of Christianity that came into south-east Wales with the Romans established itself particularly through the Roman *castra*, principally Caerwent. Following the Council of Nicaea in 325, the organisation of the Church generally followed the organisation of the Roman Empire, with a city having a bishop covering the area that came under the city's jurisdiction. The episcopal area of the earliest named bishop for south-east Wales, Dubricius or Dyfrig (*c*.465–*c*.550), obviously included Llanilltud as he ordained Samson as deacon and priest here, according to the seventh-century *Vita Samsonis*, and later as bishop. Dubricius' episcopal area perhaps extended as far west as Caldey in west Wales, for the *Vita Samsonis* tells how he appointed Samson cellarer of the monastery there. In the twelfth-century *Vita Iltuti* it is Dubricius who gives Illtud the monk's tonsure and marks out Llanilltud for him. Dubricius attended the synod at Llanddewi Brefi in 545, which was called to combat the revival in the Pelagian heresy, at which he seems to have transferred the western part of his episcopal area to David's diocese.

Although there is no documentary evidence to show who appointed and consecrated Dubricius as bishop, there were bishops in Britain in the fourth century, as it is recorded that the Bishops of York, London and probably Lincoln attended the Council of Arles in 314. These would not have been the only bishops at the time, but were the ones who had acquired metropolitical status by having jurisdiction within the capital of a province. It is therefore likely that Dubricius was not the first bishop in south-east Wales. The connection of the bishops with the continental Church was such that they could seek help from the bishops of Gaul to deal with the Pelagian heresy. Later, however, the relative isolation of the Church in Britain and its tendency to go its own way led to the concerns of Pope Gregory the Great, who sent Augustine on his mission to "a barbarous, fierce and pagan nation" in 597,[64] and then to the Synod of Whitby in 664. These two events do not seem to have immediately impacted on the Welsh Church; indeed it did not conform to the decisions made by that Synod until a hundred years after it was held.

The frequent references to St Illtud being a disciple of St Germanus in the various Lives illustrates how important it was to show that the monastic school at Llanilltud was teaching in the orthodox Catholic tradition. The threefold Order of bishops, priests and deacons, the centrality of the Eucharist, the use of liturgical forms, and the celebration of saints' feast days are all reflected in the pattern of life at Llanilltud as seen in the *Vita Samsonis*. The community at Llanilltud was established in the late fifth century not as part of a distinctive Celtic Church but of the Romano-British Church dating back to the early fourth century. This had established an episcopal structure and a liturgical base, though – as we will see – with their own distinctive characteristics.

The site of Llanilltud

It is believed by many that the prefix *Llan* in a place name means 'Church of', sometimes with a mutation (change of initial consonant) in the first letter of the saint's name which follows

– so, for example, Llandeilo is thought to mean 'The Church of St Teilo' and Llandyfodwg, 'The Church of St Tyfodwg'. Confusion may be caused by the realisation that there is no St Taff, but Llandaff is thought to mean 'the Church on the Taff'; and of course there is no St Twit because Llantwit is a corruption of Llanilltud.

However *llan* does not refer to the church but to the enclosed land around the church. This would normally be the burial ground or, in the case of a monastic community, the land within its boundaries. While the historical value of the twelfth-century *Vita Iltuti* can be disputed, the writer's description of the process by which Illtud set up his *llan* seems plausible:

> building at once first a habitation, marking out the boundary of a cemetery, and in the midst, in honour of the supreme and undivided Trinity, the foundation of an oratory... These having been duly marked out, he founded a church, a quadrangular rampart of stone being made above the surrounding ditch.[65]

St Illtud's *llan* would have been quite extensive because contained within it was a school for young pupils, a college to train priests and missionaries, a monastery with individual cells for the monks, communal areas such as a refectory, and a farm. Iolo Morganwg's claim of 2,000 students at Llanilltud may be an exaggeration – we must never rely on him to be at all historically accurate – but the activities at Llanilltud would suggest that a reasonable number of people would have been within the *llan*. No buildings remain at Llanilltud from the early medieval period, so one can only speculate, but in Ireland the monastic 'cities' such as Glendalough and Clonmacnoise covered a considerable area to accommodate the monks, lay brothers, married families, students and pupils. We do not know the composition of St Illtud's community – that is, whether there were hermits living a solitary life alongside the monks living in community, whether there were families living alongside the celibate – though the indications in the

45

Vita Samsonis are that there was a variety of monks, priests and lay, living under a variety of disciplines.

The only description of the site of St Illtud's *llan* comes in the twelfth-century *Vita Iltuti*, which tells us that, following the visitation of an angel, Illtud made his way to a valley:

> called Hoddnant, which not without reason means in Latin *vallis prospera*, prosperous valley. About it stood no mountains or steep unevenness, but a most fertile open plain. There was a very thick wood, planted with diverse trees, which was the crowded abode of wild beasts. A very pleasing river laved its two banks, and wells intermixed with rills along their pleasing courses. After he had rested and examined everything, the delectable spot pleased him, as the angel had indicated before in dreams. Here is the woody grove, a sunny spot to those who tarry there; here too about the plains is rich fertility. Through the midst there runs a flowing stream of waters. This I know may be said, it is the most beautiful of places.[66]

The stream running through the east of Llantwit Major still bears the name Hoddnant; but the description from the *Vita Iltuti* fits the valley of the Afon Colhuw into which the Hoddnant and Ogney brooks flow. Does this mean that Illtud's monastic school was here, rather than where the present St Illtud's Church is?

On the east cliff of the beach and mouth of Afon Colhuw is the large Iron Age promontory fort, named 'Castle Ditches' on Ordnance Survey maps. Archaeological finds, including querns, rubbing stones, sling stones and pottery, suggest that it was constructed between *c.*100 BC and *c.*120 AD. It would seem that, in common with other such forts, because there is no evidence of human occupation, it would have been used as a temporary refuge during attack, with its primary function to provide pounds for livestock as well an observation post. Farmers and their families would have their wattle and daub or wooden houses in the valley below, which provided a fresh water supply. The fort continued in use until the early twelfth century and was called the Castle of Meirchion, after the king Meirchion who gave Illtud the valley. King Meirchion describes the valley in the *Vita Iltuti:*

> As long as I shall reign, I shall not offend thee; most freely mayest thou hold this district. Appoint husbandmen over this territory, for this territory is meet to be cultivated, and there is none more fertile throughout the country. Tilled it abounds in harvests; it is seen to be flowing with honey and fragrant with flowers. Italy is fertile, abounding in fruits of the earth; this is more abundant and more temperate without its excessive heats. Too much cold does not destroy the crops, superfluous heat does not parch the fruits. It speedily ripens them at a suitable time; the reapers rejoice, more joyful than the reapers of Italy. Rejoice thou, therefore, to abide in such a territory; thou oughtest to rejoice, so I prophesy, for innumerable folk will rejoice in thy manner of life.[67]

The Castle of Meirchion, or Castle Ditches, was used to protect the monks and other members of the community at Llanilltud during the various Viking raids and finally during attacks by the native Welsh in 1100 before the complete subjection of the area by the Normans. The *Vita Iltuti* vividly describes the final battle at Castle Ditches:

> When William, king of the English, was reigning throughout Britain, and prince Robert fitz Hamon was ruling Glamorgan, the Northern Britons began zealously to resist the king, and afterwards in common and firm confederacy with them the Southern Britons. They wasted and burnt villages and towns. The foe came from the woods to injure their English-born and Norman- born fellow-countrymen. They laid waste and returned to distant mountains and to woods with immense plunder.
>
> In the meantime an army was put in motion by the Welsh of about three thousand armed horsemen and foot soldiers to waste and burn Glamorgan. When this was heard, the clergy of Saint Illtud with the inhabitants of their district, on account of the hostile attack, fortified themselves by means of a ditch and by means of a hedge firmly made above the sea shore, and so fortified they entered, endeavouring to protect their wealth by defence. This

47

being done, the incautious foe came by night before the gate, for if they had come by day, they would have had success. Therefore a nocturnal fight began between the two battle-fronts, until many fell dead from the hurling of stones and the vibration of spears, and others, very many, wounded, suffered greatly, groaning in the contest. Whilst such things were being done, thick sparks frequently appeared in the air between the church of Saint Illtud and the fortress of King Meirchion, near which was the battle. They shone intensely like lightning, to protect the catholic people; angelic signs they appeared to be. The more the two battle-fronts attacked, the more ardently did the fiery figures blaze in the upper air. The refuge of God and of the most holy Illtud was violated, wherefore three thousand were overcome before the fortress by a smaller number. Unarmed women administered arms to the combatants; weak boys were not inactive within. Hostile shields were broken by stones cast at them; terrific outcries were poured forth by the enemy; few were wanting bloody countenances. Divine power was present there, when the paucity of the fighters within put to flight and overcame three thousand.[68]

Coastal erosion, with frequent cliff falls, means that much of the fort and enclosures have been lost. It has been estimated that in the year 500 the land could have extended anything up to 800 metres out into the present Bristol Channel, making the fort a considerable size and providing more fertile land in the *vallis prospera* (prosperous valley) to sustain the growing community at the monastic school.

There are no archaeological remains to determine the site of Illtud's *llan* and no documentary evidence other than the clues offered in the *Vita Iltuti*. While recognising the limited historical basis on which the twelfth-century biographer was writing, the geographical descriptions have an authenticity about them. This is what we would expect from someone who was a priest of the Norman *clerus Sancti Iltuti*. The topography of the *vallis prospera*, with the present-day meadows leading down to the sea from the confluence of the Hoddnant and Ogney brooks, is just as the twelfth-century writer describes, as are the Castle Ditches.

From a reading of the *Vita Iltuti* it would seem that Illtud's *llan* was situated not where the present church is but nearer the coast in the valley of the present Afon Colhuw. Leaving aside the spurious historical references (other than the account of the battle at Castle Ditches), the description indicates that the sixth-century *llan* was situated in the broad part of the valley below the Castle Ditches – then some distance from the sea. The early founders of monasteries frequently established their communities on abandoned settlements, re-using agricultural ground and defences. The proximity of the sea, with a suitable landing place, would enable communication with other parts of the Celtic world. The river mouth of the Colhuw provided a suitable site for a port, serving the seaways to and from Somerset and further afield to Brittany and Ireland. Some remains of the port at Llantwit Major, dating back to the fifteenth century, can be seen at low tide some 200 metres from the shoreline.[69] John Leland observed during his journey through Wales between 1536 and 1539 that at "Colhow on the shore […] hither cummith sumtyme bootes and shippeleted for socuor",[70] but by the end of the sixteenth century the port had been abandoned, probably as the result of exceptional storms documented at that time.[71]

Further possible evidence of the site of Illtud's *llan* being closer to the sea than the present church is contained in the *Vita Iltuti*, where the writer describes what we would now call storm surges:

> Such agreeableness of position as the aforesaid pleased him who dwelt there, level grounds on every side surrounding a plain, and a wood unfelled between. Yet he was troubled by the frequent inundation of the sea and a fluvial approach towards his cemetery. Therefore moved by grief and fear, lest it should invade and occupy further the whole valley, he built an immense dyke, a mixture of mud and stones, which should beat back the inrushing wave, that was wont to swell beyond measure, the river only having room to flow to the sea through the middle of it. After the work was done, the force of the waves broke the dyke. A second

time he renovated it, and the second operation the surge broke anew. A third time he repeated the task, nor did the repetition avail, but came to ruin. Saint Illtud grieved, saying such words as these, 'Here I will dwell no longer; most willingly I might wish it, but troubled on account of this marine molestation I shall not be able. It will destroy my buildings, it will flow into the oratories which we constructed laboriously'.[72]

Illtud is forbidden by angelic voices to withdraw from the *vallis prospera* and as we have seen, unlike King Canute, drove back the sea with the result that marshy land having become dry was fertile for agriculture, and what was not arable, the clergy had in meadow, with fodder in abundance for cattle.

As we have noted, this story reflects the similar one in the *Vita Pauli Aureliani*, written at Saint-Pol-de-Léon in Brittany in the late ninth century:

> The place which they call the Monastery of Iltut was of very limited area and hemmed in by the sea. The four disciples (St Paul Aurelian, St David, St Samson and St Gildas) asked their master to pray to the Lord that he might cause the sea to retire, and so enlarge his domain. Iltut agrees and goes apart to pray.... then, accompanied by his disciples, he went down to the shore at low tide, when the sea used to withdraw to the distance of a mile or more, and traced, with the point of his staff, a furrow, beyond which he forbade the water to pass, and it has never since that time transgressed his command. The land which was thus reclaimed from the sea is exceedingly fertile, and never ceases, to this day, to yield abundant crops for the monastery of the aforesaid master.[73]

Because there is no evidence from within the *Vita Pauli Aureliani* or from external sources that its Breton writer Wrmonoc ever visited Llanilltud, it is likely that he heard this and other stories of Illtud from Welsh visitors to Saint-Pol-de-Léon and the area, which had a close relationship with south Wales, as evidenced by dedications to St Illtud and St Cadoc in northern Brittany. So this could be a story handed down from an early tradition, though it is not mentioned in the seventh-century *Vita Samsonis* – even though Samson is said in the *Vita Pauli Aureliani* to have been one of Illtud's disciples present at the time. The seventh-century writer may not have seen it as relevant to his story, or else he was simply not aware of the tradition. Storm surges are not uncommon along the Bristol Channel. For example, the combination of 90 mph winds and high tides in early 1990 caused severe damage to the sea wall and Lifeguard Clubhouse at Llantwit Major, with flooding in the meadows of the Afon Colhuw. The famous wave surge up the Bristol Channel on 30 January 1607 killed 2,000 people and caused extensive flooding and destruction of buildings. There are records of storms between 1550 and 1600 with exceptional high tides, resulting in the destruction of the port, and also between 1150 and 1250. It is extremely likely that there were similar wave surges, exceptional high tides and storms that caused the inundation of the sea into Illtud's *llan* and its subsequent, perhaps sudden withdrawal, which may have led to the legend of Illtud driving back the waves.[74]

The lack of archaeological evidence of St Illtud's *llan*, either in the valley of the Afon Colhuw or at the present site of St Illtud's Church in Llantwit Major, means that we can only conjecture about its location. While we might surmise on the basis of the description of the battle at Castle Ditches that it may have moved further inland following the battle, and perhaps that its apportionment by Tewkesbury Abbey resulted in the building of the present West Church of St Illtud's, it is more likely to have been moved earlier. Frequent raids by Irish pirates and Vikings are recorded along the south Wales coast; because of its exposed position from the seaward side, as a result the community may have moved inland to the more secluded valley of the Ogney brook. This may have coincided with royal patronage from the kings of Glywysing and the commissioning of memorial crosses such as the Houelt Cross,

51

now in the Galilee Chapel of St Illtud's Church. The architect G.E. Halliday, who restored St Illtud's Church in 1898 and 1905, conjectured that a stone church was built on the site of the present West Church at the same time that the Samson or Illtud Cross, now also in the Galilee Chapel, was erected. As Halliday proved that this tenth-century cross was in its original position on the north side of the present churchyard before it was moved to the West Church in 1903, he thought that if there was a stone church on the site then it would be contemporary with the Illtud cross.[75]

The Monastic School and its pupils

Llanilltud Fawr makes claims that it is "Britain's oldest centre of learning", the "University of the Celtic Saints", "the cradle of Celtic Christianity", and that Illtud "played a significant part in bringing Christianity to Britain".[76] Other claims make Llanilltud "the Christian axis of the Celtic-speaking peoples" and the "University of the Atlantic".[77]

While one may question some of those claims, the significance of Illtud's monastic school cannot be disputed. Leaving aside for a moment the Biblical teaching pupils would have received, the *Vita Samsonis* shows that the curriculum would have included "every branch of philosophy", that is to say the sciences including geometry, "rhetoric, grammar and arithmetic".[78] The twelfth-century *Vita Iltuti* shows that Illtud's parents "vowed to dedicate him to literature, and they dedicate him so vowed to be instructed in the seven arts".[79]

As we have seen, the end of the fifth and the beginning of the sixth century was a turbulent time in Welsh history, with the fall of the Roman Empire, the conflict between the various Brythonic Celtic kingdoms of Wales, the push westward by the Anglo-Saxon kingdom of Mercia, and the attacks along the south Wales coast by Irish raiders. It would seem that the Romano-British society found at Caerwent and at other centres was being lost, including the villa at Caermead near Llantwit

Major, along with its cultural and intellectual heritage. There was also the persistent problem of Pelagianism and the need to promote orthodox Christian teaching, following the two missions of St Germanus. So through his school, Illtud was bringing a beacon of hope when all seemed to be crumbling: light in the so-called Dark Ages, offering classical education and Christian teaching; yet he was also grounded in the traditional ancient culture of the land. The *Vita Samsonis* stresses that "by birth he was a most wise magician, having knowledge of the future".[80] Thomas Taylor asks in a footnote in his translation, "Was he a Druid by birth or descent?" Illtud's prophetic powers would certainly have earned him respect from the tribal kings, if not even causing them to fear him.

The *Vita Samsonis* gives us a clear picture of life at the monastic school of Llanilltud. The story of Samson's birth is a reflection of that of St John the Baptist and even of the annunciation to the Virgin Mary. His mother, Anna, was thought to be "unfruitful and barren", "the hope of children for the woman" abandoned. God, however, spoke to her in a vision: "Blessed art thou, blessed is thy womb and blessed the fruit of thy womb." Anna was unable to respond but an angel reassured her, "Fear not... behold, thou shalt have a child and thou shalt call thy firstborn son Samson; he shall be holy and a high priest before Almighty God."[81] Anna "joyfully conceived, gladly bore and successfully brought forth the beloved of God, her first-born son. Then a mighty joy seized hold of their kinsmen when they heard this, as they gave thanks to God because the Lord turned in mercy towards them." When Samson was five years of age he "very much wished to go to the school of Christ"; it took an angel to convince his father, Amon, who thought "the office of a cleric as unworthy of his family", and so they set off on the journey to "the school of the famous master of the Britons, Eltut by name".[82]

For a young child to be sent to a Christian community to be educated was common practice. Lifris' *Vita Cadoci* tells how Cadoc, in the course of his travels in foreign lands, was implored by a queen to free her from the curse of barrenness. He interceded for her and eventually she bore a son, Elli, whom she entrusted to his charge. Cadoc brought the infant Elli to his monastic school at Llancarfan, educating him with great care. As it was likely that families lived within the *llan* or monastic enclosure, married couples would become foster-parents to the younger children. The monastic school at Llanilltud would no doubt have received a welcome income from wealthy parents, such as Samson's, who sent their children at a tender age to be educated there, which would then be used for the training and support of the monks. Samson's parents brought gifts to Llanilltud, "according to custom".[83] Land was given by the local lord: as we have seen, the twelfth-century *Vita Iltuti* tells us that it was King Meirchion who made grants of land to Illtud for agriculture, for "this territory is meet to be cultivated, and there is none more fertile throughout the country".[84] This ensured that the monastic school could be self-sufficient.

The *Vita Samsonis* details the education that Samson received at Llanilltud, which presumably followed the usual pattern. He first learnt the "twenty letters" of the alphabet, though he managed to do this in one day; then "within seven days he was able, by God's revealing, to understand the meaning of these letters in the co-ordination of words".[85] The textbook for this was the Book of Psalms, the Psalter, essential reading for anyone within the community, for the psalms formed the basis of the Divine Office. In 1914, in the Springmount bog in County Antrim, there were found wooden tablets inlaid with wax on which were inscribed, probably with a stylus, verses from Psalms 30 to 32 in Latin. These date from around the year 600 and it is thought that the tablets came from a nearby monastery and were probably used for teaching reading and as an aid for memorising the Psalms. Could something like the Springmount tablets have been used to teach Samson and other pupils at Llanilltud?

Samson's biographer does not mention the other subjects in which he says Illtud was accomplished, but jumps forward to Samson's education at fifteen years of age, when "he exercised himself in the very frequent fasts and the longer vigils which were kept by all the brothers who lived there." Pupils were obviously being prepared for the spiritual life of the community, particularly those who would later take monastic vows. Samson, in his enthusiasm, tried "to maintain the appointed posture, sometimes even for two days". This was to stand with arms outstretched in the shape of the cross; but Illtud forbade this, saying to Samson, "It is not meet, little son, that the tender body of a youth, up till now in the flowering stage, should be broken by too many and ill-regulated fasts."

Pupils would also study "the deeper meanings of the Scriptures". Typically Samson wanted to "seek for more in spiritual interpretations than was presented to him" by Illtud, and his biographer recounts an occasion when, even after "studying all the treatises of the Old and New Testaments", Samson and Illtud could not answer "a certain deep question". Samson undertook fasts and vigils for three days; on the third night the answer was given to him by a voice from heaven, and the next day he was able to "gently relate to his master" all that he had heard.[86]

That is all that we are told in the Lives about the school at Llanilltud, but it obviously had a wide reputation: the ninth-century *Vita Pauli Aureliani* and the twelfth-century *Vita Iltuti* state that Paul Aurelian (the first Bishop of Léon and one of the founder saints of Brittany, c.494–c.594), David (abbot of Menevia – now St Davids – and patron saint of Wales, c.500–c.589) and Gildas (writer of *De Excidio et Conquestu Britanniae*, c.500–c.570) also studied there, in addition to Samson.

Who were these four pupils who were said to have studied at Llanilltud? We have already been introduced to Samson, for his Life is the earliest record we have of Illtud and the monastic school. Not only was Samson educated in the 'three Rs' at

Llanilltud, but he was also trained to be a deacon and priest in the monastic discipline. He became Abbot of Llanilltud's daughter house on Caldey Island, though "as a hermit rather than as a member of an order of monks".[87] Samson was invited to go to Ireland where he founded or revived a monastery.[88] On his return, he was summoned to a synod at Llanilltud, and there ordained bishop on 22 February 521. The following Easter, Samson felt the call "to be a pilgrim" and travelled across the Severn Sea (now the Bristol Channel) to Cornwall, where he is said to have performed a number of healing miracles before seeking "the Southern Sea which leads to Europe".[89] There is a tradition that he spent some time in the Scilly Isles, where an island is named after him, and in Guernsey, where he is regarded as the patron saint. He then moved on to found his main monastery near Dol in Brittany, where he is regarded as one of the seven founding saints of that country. He is probably the *Samson peccator episcopus* (Bishop Samson the sinner) who signed the acts of a synod of bishops in Paris in 557 and died in about 565, being buried in Dol Cathedral.

Paul Aurelian is another of the founding saints of Brittany. The information board at Saint-Pol-de-Léon states that he was born at Boverton in Llantwit Major. According to his Life, the *Vita Pauli Aureliani*, which was completed in 884 by the Breton monk Wrmonoc of Landévennec Abbey, Paul was the son of the Welsh chieftain Perphirius/Porphyrius ('clad in purple') of Penychen in Glamorgan. Here, however, we run into confusion: Wrmonoc, in addition to hearing about this Paul of Penychen, had also heard about a Paulinus – by which name the founder of Saint-Pol-de-Léon is also known – who he said came from a region we now know as Carmarthenshire. This Paulinus was a hermit and teacher at a place generally believed to be Whitland. The stories of the two, Paul and Paulinus, become conflated, so we cannot be certain whether Wrmonoc has the right identification for his Paul. Wrmonoc writes. "Saint Paul, while still of tender years, asked his father to send him to the school of a certain master, who was a burning and a shining light."[90] However, he states that this master "Iltutus" lived on the island of Pyrus within the *patria* (homeland) of the Demetae (now Dyfed). This is obviously Caldey Island, which in Wrmonoc's time was named after its former abbot, Pyr (or Piro), who is mentioned in the *Vita Samsonis*. Wrmonoc describes Illtud as "a man of noble birth and great learning" who had many disciples, flocking from all over Britain. It would seem once again that Wrmonoc, who did not visit Wales, has misunderstood what he has been told: Illtud used Caldey Island as a retreat but there is no tradition of a school there.

It is interesting that in his *Vita Sancti David*, compiled towards the end of the eleventh century, Rhygyfarch writes that David "went to Paulens (or Paulinus) the scribe, a disciple of St Germanus the bishop, who in a certain island was leading a life pleasing to God, and who taught him in the three parts of reading until he was a scribe."[91] As with the authors of so many of the early medieval Lives of saints, we have to treat Rhygyfarch's historical knowledge with great caution and realise that he knew very little about David, trawling information from documents housed at St Davids Cathedral and using what he could glean and what he imagined for political ends. His father Sulien was Bishop of St Davids and was under pressure from the Norman threat to the old ecclesiastical order in Wales. Wanting to raise the status of his cathedral, diocese and patron saint, he very likely asked his son to write St David's biography with little concern for historical accuracy. Was the Paulinus that Rhygyfarch says was David's teacher the same Paulinus mentioned by Wrmonoc as a fellow pupil? Is the "certain island" Caldey? Has Rhygyfarch, like Wrmonoc, confused Caldey with Llanilltud? However, what is more significant is Rhygyfarch's statement that Paulinus was "a disciple of Saint Germanus the bishop". This would be impossible because Germanus died in 448 – but we need to remember that the *Vita Samsonis* says that Illtud was also a pupil of Germanus and that Germanus had ordained him priest, again chronologically impossible. The Germanus tradition was obviously present at Llanilltud for many centuries.

To return to Paul Aurelian: he, Samson, David and Gildas were placed in authority over the other students by Illtud and, as we have seen, joined with Illtud in the driving back of the sea, which provided more fertile land for the monastery. The description is more applicable to Llanilltud than to Caldey. This is followed in the *Vita Pauli Aureliani* by an interesting little story reflecting farming life at the monastery. Illtud commanded the four to take turns in watching the ripening crops to prevent them from being damaged by seagulls. When Paul's turn came, he did not pay sufficient attention and the seagulls swallowed all the grain. Because of his negligence, Paul was afraid to show himself at the monastery, and spent a day and night in prayer. The following day he got Samson, David and Gildas to help him drive the birds into the barn, as though they were sheep. Illtud heard of what had happened; he and the other monks fell before Paul and glorified God for what he had done through the young man, singing a song together. This story also appears in the *Vita Gildae* (Life of Gildas); and again in the *Vita Iltuti* where the hero is Samson, who prevented the birds from eating the corn in the first place by driving the birds from the corn without them flying away.

Later, Paul had Illtud's permission and approval to live as a hermit away from the monastery, and in a secluded place he was ordained priest by an unnamed bishop. In due course, at the request of a Cornish king called Mark, Paul left his retreat and came to the palace of Caer Banhed, spending some years instructing the Cornish and strengthening the Christian faith. Then he moved on to Brittany, where he established a number of monasteries, a hermitage on the Isle of Batz, off the coast at Roscoff, and finally a monastery a few miles inland at Ocismore, now Saint-Pol-de-Léon. The local lord, who had given Paul the island and land for the monastery, asked King

Childebert I of Paris to make Paul a bishop, whether he wanted to be one or not. In old age, Paul retired from his episcopacy to the Isle of Batz.

While there is no evidence that Illtud ever visited Brittany, ignoring the story of Illtud's visit and death at Dol in the *Vita Iltuti*, there are some 24 ancient churches dedicated to him there because of the fact that Samson and Paul Aurelian were his pupils.

The third pupil of Illtud listed in the ninth-century *Vita Pauli Aureliani* and the twelfth-century *Vita Iltuti* is David. He is the most familiar of the four, particularly in Wales as its patron saint; but most people's information about him is derived from Rhygyfarch's *Vita Sancti David*, which comes with the same health warning that we have applied to the Lives of other saints. Rhygyfarch claimed to have used as his sources books in the library of St Davids Cathedral dating from the eighth century onward that were "eaten away by the constant devouring of moths and the yearly boring of ages through the hours and seasons, and written according to the old style of the ancients",[92] and no doubt also drew on local tradition. However, he would have been selective in order to promote the political ambitions of the diocese of St Davids to be an archiepiscopal see; and in any case stories would have been changed over the centuries in their retelling. We have noticed the discrepancy between the *Vita Pauli Aureliani* and the *Vita Iltuti* on the one hand and the *Vita Sancti David* on the other as to where David went to school, and we cannot say for certain which account is correct. Did Llanilltud in later years claim David as one of its pupils in order to boast about its importance, particularly at times both in the ninth century and in the early twelfth when its fortunes were severely declining?

Rhygyfarch's description of David's monastery at *Vallis Rosina* (Rose Valley) is probably the most useful part of his work to us in understanding the life of an early medieval monastic community such as Llanilltud, and so we will return to that later. David became renowned as a teacher and preacher, credited with founding monastic communities and churches particularly in west Wales, and having an influence in Cornwall, Brittany and Ireland. However, it is extremely unlikely that David visited Jerusalem to be consecrated archbishop, as Rhygyfarch claims he did;[93] excellent propaganda by way of what we would now call 'fake news'. Perhaps the most well-known story of David is the miracle of Llanddewi Brefi, where it is said a hillock rose under David's feet, allowing him to speak to those assembled for the synod. The famous final words of David come not from Rhygyfarch's Life but from a Welsh Life of David by an anchorite of Llanddewi Brefi, written in 1350:

> *Arglwydi, vrodyr, a chwioryd, Bydwch lawen a chredwch ych ffyd a'ch cret, a gwnewch y petheu bychein a glywyssawch ac a welsawch gennyf i.*
>
> (Lords, brothers and sisters, be happy and keep your faith and your belief, and do the little things that you have heard and seen me do.)[94]

The fourth of Illtud's illustrious pupils was Gildas, noted most for his historical work *De Excidio et Conquestu Britanniae* (On the Ruin and Conquest of Britain), written in about 540. He was born, according to 'A monk of Rhuys', his eleventh-century Breton biographer, "in the very fertile district of Arecluta... as it forms a part of Britain, took its name from a certain river called the Clut, by which that district is, for the most part, watered". This has been identified as Strathclyde in Scotland, known in Welsh as *Hen Ogledd*, the Brythonic-speaking region of northern Britain. In *De Excidio et Conquestu Britanniae*, Gildas says that "the time of my own nativity" was "the year of the siege of Badon Hill", when Ambrosius Aurelianus defeated the Saxons[95] – c.493, according to the Venerable Bede.[96] Gildas' father was Caunus, the king of Clut, "a most noble and Catholic man", who entrusted Gildas:

to the charge of St Hildutus, to be instructed by him. He took the holy child to himself, and began to teach him in sacred literature; and seeing he excelled in outward beauty, and was most eagerly bent upon the liberal studies, he loved him with tender love, and strove to teach him with attentive zeal. The blessed Gildas was, therefore, established under a master's training in the school of divine scripture and of the liberal arts.[97]

His biographer tells how Gildas developed from a boy to a youth and was "distinguished for wisdom, was constant in reading the Scriptures, ever devoted to watchings and prayers, devout in ineffable love, pleasant in action, of a winning face and handsome in all his body." His fellow pupils, Samson and Paul, are mentioned, though not David; however "the blessed Gildas surpassed even these men in the wonderful keenness of his talents."

Then are recorded two incidents that either the monk of Rhuys copied from the late ninth-century *Vita Pauli Aureliani* by his fellow Breton Wrmonoc, or else both had used an earlier source: these are the extending of the land of the monastery and the driving of the birds away from the cornfields. Llanilltud is described in the *Vita Gildae* as "a certain island, narrow, confined and squalid with its arid soil": once again it would seem to be a confusion with Caldey. The "blessed boy Gildas" challenged his master Illtud that if he believed what he preached then God would answer his prayer and give what was beneficial: "why do you not ask our Lord Jesus Christ, who is powerful to bestow all things which are asked of Him in faith, that He extend the boundaries of this island, and make its soil fruitful?" Illtud "wondered at the boy's faith" and called together all the disciples to the oratory, praying that "the Almighty Lord... may command the boundaries of this island to extend, and impart fruitfulness to its soil, in order that unto us, Thy servants, and unto our successors, it may, through the bountifulness of Thy grace, afford food in abundance. [...] When all had said Amen, and had gone out from the oratory, they saw the island enlarged in all directions, and blossoming round about with various flowers."[98]

Then, as in the *Vita Pauli Aurelian*, the story of the driving away of the birds from the cornfields immediately follows:

> Accordingly, with wonderful virtue, the old man began to till the island thus enlarged for him, and to sow seeds of corn in the fertile fields. When the glad buds of the fruits began to sprout, the sea birds flocked together and began to destroy them. On seeing this, the father Hildutus commanded his disciples to scare and drive them away, and each of them in his own day, to guard the cornfields.

In this version, it is once again Paul who failed to scare the seagulls, but not because he did not concentrate on his task. On the day of his turn:

> there arrived, in greater numbers than usual, a hostile throng of birds, which kept devastating the cornfield everywhere by plucking the ears of corn. Paul, however, a youth of wonderful activity, kept running hither and thither, shouting loudly, and strove his best to scare them away, but did not succeed. At last then, quite worn out, he called his comrades to his aid, even Gildas of blessed memory, and the venerable Samson, rousing them with words to this effect: help me, brethren, help me, most beloved brethren [...] At this word his comrades flew to his help; and the holy boys, after calling upon the name of Christ, gathered together the multitude of wild birds, and then, filled with the power of God, drove them before them like flocks of idle sheep.

The seagulls "departed far away, and no further presumed to lay waste the cornfields in that island. That island is called, up to this day, Llanilltud (the Llan of Illtud)".[99]

Gildas spent some years being taught by Illtud "both in secular writings, as far as the subject demanded, and in divine writings", and then left for Ireland for further instruction and was ordained priest. He travelled through Ireland and northern Britain, teaching and establishing churches; he supposedly visited Rome and Ravenna, according to his biographer; then finally settled in Brittany, founding the monastery of Rhuys. It was there that Gildas wrote his *De Excidio et Conquestu Britanniae*, which recounts the sub-Roman history of Britain, the only substantial source for the history of this period that is written by someone of the time. The Venerable Bede drew upon Gildas' work for the first book of his *Ecclesiastical History of the English People*.

Gildas died on 29 January, probably in the year 570. While we have to approach the biography by the 'monk of Rhuys' with as much scepticism as other Lives of saints, there are enough elements in it to build up a picture of life at Llanilltud. A twelfth-century Life of Gildas by Caradoc of Llancarfan does not mention St Illtud, Gildas studying instead in Gaul. St Cadoc invites Gildas to teach at his monastery at Llancarfan for a year, which he does, also inscribing a Gospel Book which becomes a prize possession of the monastery and renowned throughout Wales; Gildas then retires to an island for seven years before ending up in Glastonbury, building a hermitage there. Caradoc says that Gildas was "buried in the middle of the pavement of St Mary's Church [Glastonbury]; and his soul rested, rests, and will rest, in heavenly repose."

While no other Llanilltud pupil is named in the various Lives, there are a number of churches – especially in Glamorgan – which have dedications to saints who local tradition says studied under Illtud. Crallo, to whom the church at Coychurch near Bridgend is dedicated, is said to have been a nephew of Illtud. Crallo's mother was Canna, commemorated at Llangan, the parish adjoining Coychurch. Isan, commemorated at Llanishen, Cardiff and Llanishen in Monmouthshire, is the Isanus of the *Vita Samsonis* who was present at Illtud's death. Gwynno and Tyfodwg, along with Illtud, are commemorated at Llantrisant, whose name means the '*llan* of the Three Saints'. As missionary disciples of Llanilltud, the tradition is that Gwynno founded a *llan* and its community at Llanwynno near Pontypridd, and Tyfodwg founded one at Llandyfodwg, now in Bridgend County, and another at Ystradyfodwg in the Rhondda Valley.

The 'llan' of Llanilltud

Illtud would perhaps have chosen the *vallis prospera* (prosperous valley) as the site of his *llan* because there was already a nascent Christian community in the Hoddnant Valley, but also because it was "a most fertile open plain" with plenty of trees for use as building materials and for fires, a river and wells for water, and ease of access from sea and land; in addition, the defences of the Castle Ditches (the old Iron Age fort) provided a refuge to which the community could retreat with their livestock in case of attack.

It was important for a *llan* to mark out its territory to prevent disputes with its neighbours – and there were disputes aplenty if we are to believe the later biographers: Illtud was often in dispute with King Meirchion, who the *Vita Iltuti* tells us gave him the land in the first place – but also for more practical reasons, to prevent the cattle and sheep of the community from straying. The *Vita Iltuti* says that the boundary was of stone – as indeed it was at other later monasteries such as Lindisfarne, according to Bede – but it was more likely to have originally been of stakes or a hedge.

Buildings would have been simply constructed of wood, wattle and daub. Each individual within the *llan* would have his own hut in which he lived and slept; the *Vita Samsonis* implies that the monks ate together, probably in a refectory.[100] The oratory to which the *Vita Iltuti* refers would also have been simple and constructed of wood, as would the later church. Indeed, as we may infer from a drawing in the early ninth-century *Book of Kells*,[101] the church in the earliest monasteries may have just been large enough to provide a shelter for the altar and the priest saying Mass, with the congregation standing outside. Even in the later monasteries, the churches were not large, and indeed there could have been a number within the enclosure: at St Ciaran's monastery in Ireland, Clonmacnoise, there were eight churches; and at St Kevin's monastery, Glendalough, there were seven. It was not always even deemed necessary to have a special building for worship, for a simple cross might be erected with the priest setting up a portable altar at its foot. Manuscripts record a number of saints having portable altars: Rhygyfarch tells us that David's was given by the patriarch of Jerusalem, while Cuthbert's more modest wooden altar is on display in Durham Cathedral.

In addition to a portable altar, another essential item for a monk to carry was a bell to summon people to worship. A bell called Cloc ind Édachta, on display in the National Museum of Ireland in Dublin, is reputed to have belonged to St Patrick, and about fifty others from the sixth to tenth century are attributed as belonging to Irish saints. We can assume that Illtud had a bell, though in his usual manner, the author of the twelfth-century *Vita Iltuti* made a story out of it. As a result of one of his disputes with King Meirchion, he says Illtud had to flee, hiding in "a very secret cave" on "the bank of the river Ewenny" for "the space of one year and for the space of three days and nights in addition".[102] Illtud "was diligently looked for in woods and in forests, and in the retreats of deep valleys, and was not found after assiduous searchings".[103] However, "a certain wayfarer passed by, who was a messenger of Gildas the historian, carrying a brazen bell made by the same Gildas, that he might bear it for presentation to saint David, the bishop, in memory of past fellowship and love." Illtud, on hearing the "sweet sound" of the bell, enquired of the messenger where he was taking the bell and was told that it was going to St David by order of "the renowned Gildas". When the messenger arrived at David's monastery and presented him with the bell, it made no sound. David asked whether anyone had tried to ring it on the way and, hearing of the encounter with Illtud, said, "'I know that our master, Illtud, wished to possess it for

65

the sweetness of its sound, but he was unwilling to ask for it, hearing that it was to be sent to me by the donor, Gildas. God is unwilling that I should have this. Return without delay to the cave, and restore to Saint Illtud the thing meant for him which he desired.'" The messenger gave it to Illtud, then returned to Llanilltud, and related what had happened. The monks went to the cave that the messenger had discovered, found Illtud, and brought him back home to Llanilltud.

There are obvious geographical and historical inaccuracies in this story. The cave in which Illtud hid was so secret that no one has been able to identify it even to this day, and it certainly has not been located close to the River Ewenny. St David founded his monastery no earlier than 550, some thirty years after Illtud's death, and there is no evidence that he was consecrated bishop.

However, this was not the end of the story of St Illtud's bell as far as the writer of the *Vita Iltuti* was concerned. He tells how "Edgar, king of the English, moved by raging fury, moved his army on account of the disobedience of the Glamorgan folk and led it to that same region, violating the territories of the saints and their very churches, and leaving not a homestead inviolate throughout the whole of that country."[104] This would seem to be Edgar I, known as Edgar the Peaceful, who was King of England from 959 to 975. St Illtud's bell was taken from his church, fastened to the neck of a horse, and carried off to England along with the other spoils of war, which were divided up at the king's encampment on the Golden Mount, probably in Somerset. While the king was resting, he had a dream of a soldier piercing his breast with a spear. Realising that he had sinned in plundering, "full of dread he bade his sacrilegious army to restore to God and to the most holy Illtud all the plunder". The horse that had brought the bell to Edgar went of its own accord back across the Severn, followed by all the other horses, lured by the sound of the bell.

Then speedily along beaches, mountains, and woods it reaches where was the way to Glamorgan, all the horses hearing and following the sweet sound. And so when the horses had reached the bank of the River Taff, the sound of the bell was heard by the clergy. Whereupon the clergy were merry, and came to meet the horse, which went before and bore forward that same little bell as far as the door of the Church of Saint Illtud. When he had brought it, he placed it down on the spot, being loosened roughly from his neck, and it fell on a stone, and by the fall it received a fracture of one part, which is shown to this day in remembrance of this extraordinary miracle. Then was glorious psalmody sung in the choir; how great were the joys and laudations on account of this miracle! [...] By such means, for the love of Illtud, God sent back the stolen bell, and the whole of the plunder to the most sacred church of the same.

The writer tells how the clergy quarrelled as to who should have which horse, each wanting the horse that had carried the bell. "This contention persisted without agreement till the morrow, almost giving rise to the murder of many." However, the next day "when they were dividing them, they perceived that all the horses were equal, and that not one excelled the rest, as they had observed previously. Then the division was concluded agreeably, and the clergy were pacified by the peaceful distribution."

This second story of St Illtud's bell, which would seem to have been at Llanilltud at the time of writing, was probably invented by the author of the *Vita Iltuti* to explain why there was a piece missing and also to warn against robbing churches, for King Edgar "departed from this life on the ninth day as punishment for his wickedness." The bell was obviously a venerated possession of Llanilltud, as indeed were the hand bells of other saints elsewhere. The bell reputed to have belonged to St Patrick had a specially designed reliquary, a bell shrine, made for it. This is dated to 1091–1105 and was commissioned by Domhnall Ua Lochlainn, King of Ireland. It can also be seen in the National Museum of Ireland in Dublin.

The appointment of the abbot

As we have seen, the twelfth-century *Vita Iltuti* implies that Illtud was appointed *magister* (master or teacher) by Bishop Dubricius, confirmed by King Meirchion: "Magistral care has been granted thee by the bishop, this also I concede and confirm by royal grant."[105] The writer is reflecting the method of appointment in his own time, when the Norman pattern of ecclesiastical organisation was taking hold with appointments being made by the bishop and confirmed in charters by the Norman lord. The seventh-century *Vita Samsonis* makes no mention of the bishop in Illtud's appointment, noting simply that he was a 'disciple' of St Germanus[106] and that Illtud followed his tradition "in the monastery which, it is said, had been founded by St German[us]".[107]

Bishops at the time of Illtud either lived in monasteries, which they had perhaps founded or had been invited to reside in by the abbot, or lived elsewhere and provided the necessary sacramental and pastoral ministry to a community. An example of the former is at the monastery at Kildare in Ireland, founded by St Brigid at about the same time as Llanilltud. Brigid discovered a priest, Conleth, living as a hermit nearby and invited him to be the priest and confessor for her community, and in about 490 he became bishop. He was described by Cogitosus, in his Life of Brigid, as "bishop of the monks of Kildare". Dubricius seems in the *Vita Samsonis* to appear at Llanilltud only when necessary for ordinations and counselling. He ordained Samson deacon at Llanilltud, at the same time ordaining two others as priests; and then a year later ordained him priest. Samson's consecration as bishop also took place at Llanilltud, again by Dubricius, along with two other bishops whose names are not recorded.

It was the monastery that was at the heart of the ecclesiastical structure in the Church in the Celtic lands, so bishops became subordinate to the abbot in the hierarchy – though, as we see from the *Vita Samsonis*, they were treated with great reverence and respect. Local rather than regional church organisation reflected the secular culture of small settlements under local tribal rule. The twelfth-century *Liber Landavensis* and the *Vita S. Dubricii* (Life of St Dubricius) contained within it give the impression that the Diocese of Llandaff existed from Dubricius' time: the latter relates that Dubricius "visited the residence of St. Illtyd, in the season of Lent, that he might correct what wanted amendment, and confirm what should be observed. [...] The business of the house of St. Illtyd was divided between the brethren; the ecclesiastical affairs were performed by such persons as they best suited, and the offices were distributed among the brethren."[108] However, this was written to strengthen the claim of the diocese over the twelfth-century *clas* (community) of Llanilltud and its lands, by showing that Llanilltud was always subject to the episcopal authority of the Bishop of Llandaff.

The ecclesiastical structure within the Church in what are now Wales, Ireland and Scotland was a contributing factor in the disputes with the Roman Church that led to the Synod of Whitby in 664, and was not resolved until the Normans imposed the diocesan structure. Bede writes of the community on the Scottish island of Iona that it "is always ruled by an abbot in priest's orders, to whose authority the whole province, including the bishops, is subject."[109] It is the abbots who are recorded in the dealings of the communities with the tribal chiefs, not the bishops – certainly in the case of Illtud and Cadoc. Sometimes it was seen as useful for an abbot to be ordained bishop: Samson was helped in his cause in Cornwall and Brittany by being a visiting bishop. The abbot ruled the monastery autocratically: there is no sense of decisions being made by consensus through the Chapter as in the later Benedictine communities.

Because the structure of the monastic community reflected the local tribal structure, the right of succession of the ruler within the monastery was hereditary, strengthened by the fact that the founder was very often from the nobility. While the *Vita Samsonis* does not tell us anything of Illtud's parentage, the author is concerned to show that Samson "as regards worldly rank was born of distinguished and noble parents". His father, Amon, was from Dyfed and his mother, Anna, was from Gwent; they were both from within the royal courts, where their parents "were court officials of the kings of their respective provinces".[110] By the twelfth century, Illtud had acquired noble status in the eyes of his biographers, either as a captain of the guard in the royal household or indeed as a cousin of King Arthur and a knight of the Round Table. As we have seen, the *Vita Iltuti* states that Illtud's father was a soldier and his mother was the daughter of the King of Britannia. Typically, the twelfth-century biographer of St Cadoc ensures that his saint is of a higher standing than Illtud by making Cadoc the son of Gwynllyw, the King of Glywysing, the kingdom covering Gwent and Glamorgan, and making his wife Gwladus, "born of most noble lineage", the daughter of a local chief, Brychan.

We are not told in the twelfth-century *Vita Iltuti* that Illtud had any offspring from his marriage to Trynihid; indeed the writer would not want to further complicate the argument for Illtud's celibacy once he had become a monk by bringing children into the matter. However, according to the *Vita Samsonis*, Illtud did have nephews, one of whom was a priest in the monastery and the other a lay brother. They were jealous of Samson, "wickedly fearing lest, on account of one whom they knew to be better than themselves, they would be deprived of a hereditary worldly possession".[111] The one who was a priest feared that "he himself would be robbed of his hereditary monastery, which he hoped to possess after his uncle".[112] There ensues plotting and scheming, with an attempt to poison Samson: the lay brother first trying the poison out on a cat by putting a little in its milk. The test proved successful, for the cat, "when it drank it in milk, it gave a headlong spring and forthwith was dead". The lay brother "was highly pleased, and doubted not that when St Samson had drunk from the vessel, he would straightway take his departure from this world." However, "the Spirit of God revealed to Samson these things and the evil of late wrought against him"; Samson trusted the words of the Gospel that "If [the faithful] shall drink any deadly thing, it shall not hurt them [...] and making the sign of the Cross on his vessel, without any wavering of mind drank it dry and never felt even the slightest heartache from it." The priest brother repented of his part in this, but the lay brother persisted "in the stubbornness of his wicked opinion". The next Sunday, when he received the bread of the Mass, the lay brother went into convulsions then stripped off his clothes and berated the other brothers. He was seized, bound and led outside. The priest brother told the community what they had done, begged for forgiveness and promised to "do penance all his life and evermore serve God and St Samson".[113] The lay brother is described as a "demoniac... vexed by the evil spirit"; Samson feared "to be present in the sight of that man who unjustly hates me" but nevertheless prayed for his healing and gave him blessed oil mixed with water. The lay brother recovered from "the devilish attack", acknowledged the evil he had done and expressed penitence; "and so, by the just judgement of God it came to pass that, while he covetously and unrighteously laid claim to the primacy, throughout his life he never held it."[114]

This episode, reported to the author of the *Vita Samsonis* by the monks at Llanilltud and alive in its memory almost a century after it is supposed to have happened, illustrates the rivalry that took place in the monastic communities and the desire to be abbot, a position which had more significance than just being the head of the community. The author provides graphic details of the effect on the lay brother of his attempted murder of Samson as a warning to those who would aspire to a position to which they were not entitled, or for which they did not have the sanctity in the eyes of God and the respect of their fellow monks.

It does not seem that there were any other relatives of Illtud that could be appointed abbot on his retirement or death, for the elders of Llanilltud "appointed St Samson abbat against his will in the monastery".[115] Leaving aside their recognition of Samson's ability and spiritual depth, it was necessary to appoint an abbot who had the necessary noble status so that the standing of the community should not be lowered in the sight of their secular counterparts. In the Irish monastic laws from about 440 onwards, the right of succession is clearly laid out: firstly a son of the abbot, then someone from the tribe of the founding saint of the community, as long as he was fitting for the position. This seems also to have been the pattern in Wales.

The spirituality of the monastery

In the last few decades, 'Celtic Christian spirituality' has sought to recover the essence of belief and practice of the pre-Norman period in the Brythonic Celtic areas of the west of Britain, though often with a romantic view which cannot be sustained through historical investigation: the alleged purity of the Celtic saints, their simplicity of life, their communing with nature. Many modern reflections, prayers and meditations that are claimed to be based on the Celtic Christian tradition are derived not from the pre-Norman period but from the *Carmina Gadelica* (Songs of the Gaels), the collection compiled by Alexander Carmichael (1832–1912), using prayers he discovered in the Gaelic-speaking Scottish Western Isles, especially the Isles of Uist. Perhaps the most accessible selection of prayers from the *Carmina Gadelica* is *The Celtic Vision* by Esther de Waal.[116] The editorial note sees de Waal's book as "introducing the Celtic people to a wider audience", showing "the unique marriage between the everyday and the eternal which marks the Celtic mind. Praying and working are not separated, and the rhythm of each day and year is celebrated and offered to God. The instinctive Celtic reverence for nature as God's creation has much to teach us today, and its everyday holiness can bring insight and inspiration to contemporary dwellers in an industrial society."

However, the prayers in the *Carmina Gadelica* were based on the oral tradition of the Western Isles, reworked by Carmichael to show the spiritual respectability of the crofters at a time when there was political unrest following the Clearances and open contempt for the Gaelic language and culture. How far back in Hebridean tradition the prayers go is a matter of debate, but it is important to stress that these have become the basis of current popular Celtic Christian spirituality rather than anything coming out of pre-Norman Wales. This is not to dismiss the attractiveness of the writings of the most popular author in this tradition, Canon David Adam[117] – vicar of Lindisfarne from 1995 to 2003 – and the spiritual benefit that one may derive from them; however these must not be seen as being derived from ancient Celtic Christian spirituality but rather from the spiritual tradition found in the *Carmina Gadelica*. To understand the Welsh Celtic Christian spirituality from before 1100 we have to go back to the Lives of the saints, recognising the historical difficulties presented by the later ones and the limited corpus of extant Welsh spiritual writing. The difference in approach is that what we know of the early Welsh spirituality is based on our understanding of the monastic life of places such as Llanilltud, in contrast to the spirituality of ordinary people such as the nineteenth-century Hebridean crofters that we find reflected in the *Carmina Gadelica* and presented so often today as 'Celtic Christian spirituality'.

The *Vita Samsonis*, the only primary source from which we could gain any indication of the spirituality of Llanilltud, does not provide us with many clues other than the round of worship based on the Daily Offices and the Eucharist. What the author of the *Vita Samsonis* shows are Samson's attempts to achieve spiritual perfection through the monastic discipline and his growing frustration as he finds Llanilltud "turbulent and indeed wasteful".[118] However, this is not the personal view of the author, who describes Llanilltud as "splendid",[119] describing how the brothers kept "very frequent fasts and longer vigils"[120] – with which, as we have seen, Samson joined in at the age of 15 until Illtud stopped him doing this.

Following his ordination as deacon, probably at the age of 23, Samson was "ever bent on fasting and exercised in unceasing prayers, also very immersed in searching and in learning the Holy Scriptures, without any pause he went on praying, according to the exhortation of the Apostle Paul, in cold and nakedness, all night long, through wintry frosts, subdued not by the winds of winter or by the very oppressive heat of summer, mindful of the Apostle's word when he says, 'the sufferings of this present time are not worthy to be compared with the glory which shall be revealed in us'".[121] His biographer comments, "In truth, St Samson had grown so wonderful and, if I may speak, so ineffable in the work of God, that from day to day, naturally rising as by a spiritual ladder higher and higher to the highest summit of religion, he was seen to emerge, by daily use, renewed and bettered."[122] Following his ordination to the priesthood, Samson "cultivated himself by a stricter rule of abstinence according to the word of the Holy Scriptures".[123] He was chaste, he was a vegetarian, and he was never drunk. Samson seemed to have tolerated Llanilltud only "for the sake of charity", eating with the rest of the community until, "ever desiring to tread that evangelical and narrow path which leads to heaven, [he] gave much thought how he might escape from the society of that brotherhood without wounding the feelings of its master."[124] Illtud realised Samson's desire to leave Llanilltud and allowed him to go to the monastery on Caldey Island, where, "leading with untiring patience, a wonderful, isolated and above all a heavenly life, he ceased not, day or night, from prayer and communion with God",[125] even to the extent of not sleeping in a bed, but resting against a wall "or anything hard for support".

As we have seen, there were three functions within the *llan* of Llanilltud: a school, a training college and a monastic community. From what we read of St Samson's spiritual journey in the *Vita Samsonis*, there was tension between those who wished to keep a rigorous spiritual discipline in isolation from the world around and those who, while keeping fasts and vigils, maintained relations with wider society. This led to Samson leaving community life at Llanilltud to become an ascetic at Caldey. Even there, he seems to have been dissatisfied with the life of the rest of the community, for when he was elected abbot following the death of its founder, Piro – who fell down a well while drunk – he "trained the brothers gently to the proper rule". But even as abbot, Samson stood apart from the rest of the community, who "regarded him as a hermit rather than as a member of an order of monks." During "feasts of plenty and flowing bowls, he made a point of fasting always from food and drink".[126]

Samson would probably not have been the only monk to have left Llanilltud either permanently or for a short period of time to become a hermit. The tradition of living a solitary life can be traced back to the earliest times, when people like Paul of Thebes (third century) and Anthony of Egypt (fourth century) withdrew to the desert. The monasticism that spread to Britain was very much influenced by the idea of withdrawal to a desert place, which was seen as the ultimate goal in spiritual life, though people had to find their own *diserth* or wilderness place in dense woodland, caves or islands. According to his twelfth-century biographer, Illtud withdrew from Llanilltud on two occasions: on the first to a cave near the River Ewenny to escape from persecution by King Meirchion; and on the second to a cave on the Gower to escape the crowds coming to Llanilltud and demanding his attention.

Unlike later monasteries that followed the Rule of St Benedict, there was not a common Rule amongst the early medieval communities in Wales; the 'proper rule' that Samson sought to impose at Caldey would have been one of his own devising. Each community would follow its own traditions, usually determined by its founder. However, there would seem to have been a common pattern of life. It was the later Rule of St Benedict that had *ora et labora* ('pray and work') as its basis; but from a reading of the *Vita Samsonis* and extrapolation from the later Lives, this was the pattern of life at Llanilltud.

Worship was central at Llanilltud, in particular the Mass and the reciting of the Psalms in the Daily Office. There are references to the singing of the Mass and "hymns and choruses and the accustomed solemnities" in the *Vita Samsonis*.[127] What form the liturgy of the Mass would have taken at Llanilltud in this period is unknown. No written text of the Mass remains before the eighth century, and in any case, each community would have developed their own words and rituals. At Llanilltud the Gospel was sung and prayer offered;[128] Communion was in two kinds; that is, both the bread and the wine.[129] The language used in worship would have been Latin, and the liturgical rite would have followed at least the framework of the Roman liturgy used on the Continent, but with a mixture of elements drawn from various sources.

The Christian Year, with all its festivals and fasts, was followed by the community. Samson is recorded as singing the Paschal (Easter) Mass at Llanilltud, as well as "the office of the Paschal Celebration".[130] Lent was observed: Bishop Dubricius went on retreat to Caldey Island for the forty days,[131] and the author of the *Vita Samsonis* writes of Samson: "Indeed we have heard that the time of the Lenten fast was so spent that at the beginning he used to withdraw from human habitations to some rather remote spot, carrying with him three loaves to suffice him until the joy of the Paschal Celebration, God supporting him in all things."[132]

It must be assumed that the monks at Llanilltud followed the canonical hours throughout the day – Lauds, Prime, Terce, Sext, None, Vespers and Compline – given that None is mentioned in the *Vita Samsonis*.[133] This pattern is found in monasteries on the Continent in the fifth century, with the recitation of psalms and scripture canticles, hymns and prayers. Later, readings from the Lives of the saints were included, particularly on their festival days. That the monks at Llanilltud kept even what might seem today to be rather obscure commemorations is seen in the *Vita Samsonis*: Samson's consecration as bishop took place on "the day of the blessed Apostle Peter's Chair",[134] which the author helpfully tells us is 22 February. This celebrates the foundation of the diocese of Antioch, the capital of the East, the chair being the one on which St Peter sat as its first bishop. There is no biblical basis for this assertion, but it is claimed by many of the early Church Fathers that St Peter was Bishop at Antioch before finally going to Rome. The commemoration is found in early Calendars, though the date was also considered to be the one on which Peter declared Jesus to be the Christ and was appointed by Christ to be the Rock of his Church.[135] According to earliest Western liturgies, 22 February became the day on which Peter was chosen as the first Pope.

It was important for the author of the *Vita Samsonis* to emphasise that there was in Llanilltud "an accustomed day when they came together for ordaining bishops", for the fact that it took place on this day of St Peter's Chair shows that St Samson was being consecrated in the apostolic tradition. This was further strengthened by Samson's vision of "himself clothed in white apparel surrounded by closest crowds of delightful beings and three distinguished bishops, wearing golden crowns on their heads", who urged him to go with them into the church. When Samson asked their names, he was told "Peter and James the Lord's brother, and John the Evangelist; the reason of their coming indeed was that they were sent by the Lord Jesus Christ to confirm him pre-eminently the chosen priest of the Lord",[136] as further proof of Samson's apostolic credentials to anyone reading the story. Peter founded the Church at Rome, James the Church in Jerusalem, and John the Church at Ephesus: so Samson had the episcopal authority both of the Church of the West and of the East.

In the second part of the *Vita Samsonis*, perhaps an epistle to be read on St Samson's festival day, the author directly addresses his readers, urging them to continue the "grand and holy and yearly celebration" of St Samson and "in the rejoicing of the festival itself, to enlarge our hearts to the greater profit of our souls".[137] The author commends the commemoration of the saints:

> Therefore, my brothers, to honour the festivals of the saints
> is nothing else than to adjust lovingly our mind to their good
> qualities, of which we are fully cognisant; [so that] by imitating
> them we may be able to follow the same men, under God's
> guidance, by the straightest course to that unspeakable and
> heavenly kingdom to which they have happily attained, not
> rivalling them in great deeds, but sharing their difficult tasks,
> which by abstinence, prolonged and incredible, so to speak, to the
> untried, with whom all things are not thought possible to him that
> believeth, they engaged in until the happy close of this life.[138]

He concludes his epistle by encouraging his readers not only to give the saints honour at their yearly festivals but also to imitate them in their manner of life, so that "while you seek to follow the doctrines which they taught and the deeds in which they unceasingly and unsparingly laboured, you may have the strength to follow, under God's guidance, and with their intercessions, by a sure course, that path of theirs which led them, without any let of earthly hindrance, to everlasting felicity, where our Lord Jesus Christ reigneth for ever."[139] It was for this reason that the Lives of the saints, such as the *Vita Samsonis*, were initially written, before they became the means for political propaganda.

The nearest we have to an outline of a liturgical form in use at Llanilltud is in the description of Samson's ordination as a deacon. Before he could be ordained, the community had to consent to his ordination; during the ceremony there was the "acclamation of all the brothers".[140] Then "the brothers were required, according to custom, to bend for pardon": this was the Litany, the preliminary to ordinations. The bishop "raised his hand over him, to confirm him as deacon", followed by the singing of the Gospel and prayer by "the one deacon who held the chalice". The tradition of the deacon as the reader of the Gospel is recorded by St Jerome before 420, and as early as the second century the deacon administered the chalice at the Eucharist. It is not certain what prayer the deacon would have recited; this could have been the invitation to the kiss of peace. Then followed "the communion of the Eucharist". The *Vita Samsonis* does not give full details of Samson's consecration as bishop; the monks consult together and agree that Samson "must be placed in the episcopal chair".[141] The writer is more concerned with the dove that stood over Samson "unmoved until he was quite through the ceremony and was ordained bishop".

Daily Life

Rhygyfarch, in his *Vita Sancti David*, details the pattern of life at Menevia. While accepting the broad picture, we must view with caution the historical accuracy of Rhygyfarch's work and the extremes of asceticism that David himself practised. The description is helpful in providing an insight into the daily life of a sixth-century monastic community such as that at Llanilltud – where, after all, David himself was perhaps trained.

At Menevia:

> every monk should toil at daily labour, and spend his life in
> common, working with his hands [...] they provided with
> their own labour all the necessities of the community [and] no
> conversation was held beyond what was necessary. But each did
> the task enjoined either with prayer or well-directed meditation
> [...] When outside labour was finished, they returned to the cells
> of the monastery, and spent the whole day till evening in reading
> or writing or praying. On the approach of evening, when the stroke

of the bell was heard, each one left his study, for if the stroke should sound in the ears of anyone, the top of a letter having been written or even half the form of that letter, they rose up the more quickly and left their tasks, and thus in silence proceeded to church without any idle talk. When the chanting of the psalms was done, the voice being in accord with the intention of the heart, they worshipped on bended knees until the stars were seen in heaven bringing the day to a close. [...] They all took supper in accordance with the varying condition of their bodies and ages [...] they provided for the sick and those advanced in age, and even those wearied with a long journey [...] after giving of thanks, they went to the church at the canonical ringing, and there they were insistent in watchings, prayers, and genuflections for about three hours [...] These things having been so done, they composed their limbs for sleep. Waking at cockcrow, they devoted themselves to prayer on bended knee.[142]

As at Menevia, so at Llanilltud did the community have "to provide with their own labour" for the needs of the monastery. If the stories in the ninth-century *Vita Pauli Aureliani* or the twelfth-century *Vita Iltuti* are to be believed, the community had considerable land that was fertile for crops, extended by the driving back of the sea, with meadows for cattle. According to the *Vita Iltuti*, "too much cold does not destroy the crops, superfluous heat does not parch the fruits. It speedily ripens them at a suitable time; the reapers rejoice."[143] As we have seen, there was also the problem of seagulls.

The monastic communities are credited with developing new techniques in farming. The plough had been developed in early times, but a number of monasteries made adaptations and innovations to make ploughing easier. For example, at St Ninian's monastery at Whithorn, parts of the plough were protected by 'plough pebbles' – stones fitted to the wooden parts of the plough to prevent them wearing away – which allowed easier movement. The Welsh Triads, a mixed collection of sayings from Welsh folklore, mythology and traditional history that were preserved in medieval manuscripts dating from the thirteenth century onwards, mention "Elltud, the holy knight of Theodosus, who improved the mode of ploughing land." Benjamin Heath Malkin, on his journey through south Wales in 1803, observed, "Illtyd is honoured by the Welsh as having introduced a plough of a construction greatly superior to any before known to the natives."[144] Rice Rees in *An essay on the Welsh saints* (1836) wrote, "The memory of Illtyd is honoured by the Welsh on account of him having introduced among them an improved method of ploughing. Before his time they were accustomed to cultivate their grounds with the mattock and over-treading plough." The St Illtud Plough was still known by that name in parishes in nineteenth-century Wales, according to *A topographical directory of Wales* (1845).

In common with many of his contemporaries like Cadoc, Teilo and Oudoceus, St Illtud is said to have had a special relationship with a stag. The *Vita Iltuti* tells how King Meirchion's hounds chased a stag, which sought refuge "inside the sleeping place of saint Illtud, as if seeking sanctuary with him after the manner of men".[145] The dogs stopped barking, remaining outside Illtud's cell. When King Meirchion rode up, he found that the stag had "become tame and domestic", but nevertheless demanded that Illtud handed it over – which of course he refused to do. Although angry, the king was "filled with respect on seeing the very great piety of the most blessed man and such great wonders performed before him in person", and allowed Illtud to keep the stag. "The same stag, tamed by saint Illtud, drew vehicles, and in the vehicles timber for building."

The popular view of Celtic Christian spirituality is that there was a unique oneness between the Celtic monk and the natural world, seeing there the immanence of God and therefore the sacredness of the earth. While there is later medieval Welsh poetry in praise of nature,[146] what emerges from the description of Llanilltud in the various Lives is the struggle against the elements, for example with the "frequent inundation of the sea",[147] and the problem with seagulls. The land had to be tamed, and it required much labour to ensure the needs of the community were met.

With a port at Llanilltud allowing an easy crossing to the West Country and further afield to Brittany and Ireland, and its proximity to the Roman road running through the Vale of Glamorgan, there must have been a constant stream of pilgrims and traders coming to the monastery. The school, community, daily round of worship, farm, and the coming and going of visitors meant Llanilltud would have been a very busy place, and of substantial size. The Irish monasteries were often referred to as cities and, although we do not have any documentary evidence of the organisation of the monastic community for the first six hundred years of its existence, we could imagine that Llanilltud resembled the *civitas* of the Romans, with a complex structure to ensure that all ran smoothly.

Pastoral Care

It has been the traditional duty of monasteries down through the centuries to provide hospitality to travellers, help for those in need and protection for those seeking sanctuary from enemies. The twelfth-century view of Llanilltud in St Illtud's time contained within the *Vita Iltuti* is that this was the case. Illtud "feeds the poor, he covers the naked, he visits the sick and those cast into prison [...] He had a hundred in his household, as many workmen, clerics, and a hundred poor persons daily. He was hospitable, most ready, never refusing hospitality to those who required it. He gave bountifully whatever was put in his hands."[148] However, the sixth-century *Vita Samsonis*, seeing Llanilltud through the prism of the life of Samson, makes no mention of the pastoral care of the monastery, not regarding this as an integral part of his life. Samson was focussed on his own spiritual journey, and it seems that he only grudgingly joined with the rest of the community for meals "for the sake of charity".[149] Even when Samson's father was "lying at death's door", Samson refused to leave Caldey, "thinking it unnecessary to return to the home in which he had been carnally born". It was Piro, the Abbot of Caldey, who had to remind Samson that he needed to have care for others.[150] Even after saying that he would quickly follow the messengers who urged him to go to his father, Samson "tarried a day and a night in the monastery after they had gone" before he undertook the journey.[151]

Pilgrimage

There is a romantic idea of the Celtic Christian setting sail in a coracle, letting the tides and winds take them wherever God wills. In essence, this was the third stage in a spiritual journey. Following on from life in a community and life as a hermit was life as a *peregrinus* (wanderer), leaving the security of one's homeland in a journey towards Christ, though often with a missionary aspect to it. As we have seen, this was the pattern that Samson's journey took. Within six weeks of being consecrated the bishop-abbot of Llanilltud, Samson left for Cornwall and eventually Brittany, having been told by an angel in a dream "of a truth thou oughtest to tarry no longer in this country, for thou art ordained to be a pilgrim".[152] It is not a journey without any end destination in mind, for Samson "directed his course towards this side of the Severn Sea";[153] that is, Cornwall. There he consecrated churches built by his mother then "eagerly sought what they call the Southern Sea, and which leads to Europe";[154] and together with his companions eventually reached "their desired port in Europe".[155]

There is no indication that Illtud left Llanilltud never to return; he was not a missionary or evangelist in the usual sense of *peregrini*. He does leave Llanilltud for a year and three days and nights according to the historically dubious *Vita Iltuti*, but that is to escape the persecution of King Meirchion.[156] On returning to Llanilltud, to the delight of his brethren, the *Vita Iltuti* tells us that "after some interval of time Saint Illtud was burdened by the multitude of people who came to him, and hindered in his prayers, for which reason he went to the cave of Llwynarth, remaining there the space of three years in vigils and fastings, receiving every ninth hour food for himself from heaven brought to him by an angel and placed on a rock within."[157] On neither occasion did Illtud travel far – it would seem to the Gower, according to local legend – though neither place can be positively identified. The story of Illtud's pilgrimage to Mont-Saint-Michel at the end of the *Vita Iltuti* is, as we have seen, obviously unhistorical.

Llanilltud was a training college for clerics, but not necessarily as missionaries. However, Samson, Paul and David (if indeed he really studied at Llanilltud Fawr) did leave to found or revive monasteries in Wales, Cornwall, Ireland and Brittany. This followed a common pattern in the early medieval monasteries in the Celtic lands, where a small group would leave to establish new monastic foundations. Samson had with him "a band of brothers" on his journey to Cornwall and Brittany;[158] Paul of Penychen, according to Wrmonoc, took his brothers Potolius and Notolius to what is now Llandovery in Carmarthenshire and established a hermitage, which grew into a monastery; David took three disciples with him, "accompanied by a great throng of fellow-disciples", to found the monastery at *Vallis Rosina*.[159] However, while there are a number of ancient churches in south Wales and one in north Wales dedicated to St Illtud, this does not necessarily mean that he or his pupils at Llanilltud founded them: they may indicate his influence many centuries later, particularly as the result of his twelfth-century biography.

The number of churches in Brittany dedicated to St Illtud would seem to be the result of Samson and Paul Aurelian's influence, out of the desire to honour their teacher. Samson (Dol) and Paul (Saint-Pol-de-Léon) are two of the seven founding saints of Brittany. It is claimed that four of the others were from Wales and, although there is no supporting evidence to prove this, that three were trained at Llanilltud Fawr: Tudwal (Treguier), a hermit from north Wales; Brioc

(Saint-Brieuc) and Patern (Vannes), from Ceredigion. The fourth, Malo (Saint-Malo) is said to have been a monk of Llancarfan. The seventh founding saint, Corentin (Quimper) is the only one who was Breton, without a Welsh connection and earlier than Illtud.

That six out of the seven Breton founding saints had Welsh origins illustrates the importance of the western sea-routes in enabling relatively easy communication between south Wales, Ireland, Cornwall and Brittany. While we can trace Samson's travels to Ireland, Cornwall and Brittany, as described in his Life, there must have been many hundreds more who set out from the port at Llanilltud Fawr or who travelled inland following the old Roman roads whose names have not been recorded, and who either established a small *llan* with travelling companions or alone founded a *diserth*, an isolated place, to devote their life to prayer.

4

LLANILLTUD FROM THE SEVENTH TO ELEVENTH CENTURY

The Welsh Church

No annals remain detailing the story of Llanilltud up until the Norman Conquest, though there are references to abbots of Llanilltud in the *Liber Landavensis* (Book of Llandaff), the twelfth-century collection of saints' Lives, charters and papal bulls. Llanilltud did not have the significance of Lindisfarne, Iona, St Davids or the Irish monasteries; it was not a place of pilgrimage as it lacked a shrine to St Illtud, so did not receive an income from travellers; no early historian of the status of the Venerable Bede wrote about it. The only archaeological evidence remaining from this period is the early medieval stones that are now housed in the Galilee Chapel of the present-day St Illtud's Church.

Gildas, a former pupil at Llanilltud, painted a depressing picture of the history of Britain and the state of the Church in his *De Excidio et Conquestu Britanniae* (On the Ruin and Conquest of Britain), written between 510 and 530. After a brief history of Britain following its conquest by the Romans and a condemnation of five British kings since that time, Gildas turned his attention to the Church: "Did I not behold such great masses of evil deeds done against God by bishops or other priests, or clerks, yea some of our own order?"[160] He then elaborated, "Britain hath priests, but they are unwise; very many that minister, but many of them impudent; clerks she hath, but certain of them are deceitful raveners; pastors (as they are called) but rather wolves prepared for the slaughter of souls…"[161] Gildas did not identify anyone by name or location but this would have provided uncomfortable reading at Llanilltud, already condemned by Gildas' fellow pupil Samson as turbulent and wasteful.

It was as a result of what was perceived as the English descent back into paganism through the Anglo-Saxon invasions that Pope Gregory the Great sent Augustine on his mission to convert the country back to Christianity, and to create an ordered system of dioceses under Augustine as Archbishop of Canterbury. Although Augustine landed in Kent in 597, it was six years before he formally met the British bishops. The delay was probably due to the bishops' suspicions about Augustine's motives in asking them to "establish brotherly relations with him in Catholic unity and to join with him in God's work of preaching the Gospel to the heathen".[162] As Bede records, "the Britons did not keep Easter at the correct time […] furthermore, certain other of their customs were at variance with the universal practice of the Church." The meeting, when it finally did happen, was at Augustine's Oak, which is traditionally said to have been at Aust on the Somerset side of the Severn Estuary, opposite Chepstow. It was attended by "seven British bishops and many very learned men", who came, Bede says, mainly from the monastery at Bangor-is-y-Coed, Clwyd, but could have included some from Llanilltud. It was Augustine's lack of humility and his refusal to accept them on equal terms, by not standing when the Welsh contingent arrived for the meeting, which determined the outcome. The bishops refused Augustine's demands, "nor would they recognise Augustine as their archbishop, saying among themselves that if he would not rise to greet them in the first instance, he would have even less regard for them once they submitted to his authority."[163] The Welsh way of organising the Church through the monasteries, with a bishop attached or at least providing the necessary sacramental functions, therefore remained until the Norman Conquest. Although the Synod of Whitby in 664 resolved differences in practice between the Northumbrian Church, centred on Lindisfarne, and Rome over the calculation of Easter and the shape of the monastic tonsure, the 'Celtic Church', centred on Iona and in Wales, retained those traditions until 716 and 768 respectively.

Abbots of Llanilltud

While a number of smaller *llannau* or monasteries would have been established in the early years by monks from Llanilltud, by the seventh century it was the three Vale of Glamorgan monasteries – Llanilltud, St Cadoc's at Llancarfan, and St Dochdwy's at Llandough – that dominated, with their abbots being frequently named in charters contained within the *Liber Landavensis*. The three abbots of the Vale of Glamorgan are mentioned in a number of charters dating to the first half of the eighth century; at this time, Cadien was the Abbot of Llanilltud.[164] Later abbots mentioned in charters include Colfryd, Elwood, Elised, Ffomreu, Cadgen and Gwrthafar, though it is difficult to determine their dates. Llanilltud seems to have diminished at least in influence in the centuries leading up to the Norman Conquest, as in charters its abbots were always ranked after those of Llancarfan.

In his *The Antiquities of Lantwit Major*, the Revd Dr David Nichols, vicar of Llantwit Major from 1661 to 1720, records a list of Abbots of Llanilltud that he found "in a loose parchment at Llandaff, very decayed and rent": Iltutus, Piro, Ifanus, Cennit, Samson, Guorthauer, Congers, Elbod, Tomre, Gwrhaval, Nudh, Eliftet, Segin, Cymelliauc, Bletri, "and many more that cannot be read now".[165] Three of these are listed in the *Liber Landavensis* as Bishops of Llandaff: Nudh, *c.*880–900;

Cymelliauc or Cyfeiliog, *c.*900–927; and Bletri, *c.*983–1022.[166] As there was not a diocese centred on Llandaff until 1120, these were probably Abbots of Llanilltud who subsequently became bishops, either operating out of their community or relocating elsewhere in the Glamorgan-Gwent area to exercise episcopal oversight. Cymelliauc is recorded in the Anglo-Saxon Chronicle as Bishop of Archenfield or Ergyng in 914, being ransomed for £40 after his capture by the Vikings; and his death in 927 is recorded in the *Liber Landavensis*, where he is styled 'Bishop of Llandaff'. Nichols writes, "it is not unlikely that Abbots of Lantwit, who were famous for holiness and learning, should be chosen by the clergy and their congregations, Bishops of Landaff and of other places; for who else could be found so properly qualified?"

An Abbot Samson, though not the Samson of the sixth century, is named on a late eighth-century pillar cross, now in the Galilee Chapel of St Illtud's Church in Llantwit Major. The inscription reads, IN NOMINE D[E]I SUMMI INCIPIT CURX SALUATORIS QUAE PREPARAUIT SAMSONIS APATIS PRO ANIMA SUA ET PRO ANIMA INUTHAHELO REX ET ARTMALI [ET] TECAI + (In the name of God the Most High being the Cross of the Saviour prepared by Abbot Samson for his soul and the soul of King Iuthahel, and of Artmael and Tecan). Various charters in the *Liber Landavensis* mention "Samson, Abbot of the altar of Saint Illtud";[167] a Samson is also mentioned in a grant by King Rotri [Rhodri], the son of Iudhail. These charters and grants have been dated to *c.*765.

Another Samson is mentioned on a cross in the Galilee Chapel, but in this case he is identified as a king: SAMSON REGIS. The cross shaft is known as the Illtud Cross, for the inscription in one panel reads + ILTU[TI] ([the cross] of Illtud). This has led some to believe it was erected by St Samson in memory of his teacher,[168] though stylistically and linguistically it is impossible for it to be any earlier than the early tenth century.

It is significant that kings' names are mentioned on three of the early medieval stones found near the present St Illtud's Church and now in the Galilee Chapel: the Samson Pillar, the Illtud Cross, and the Houelt Cross. The inscription on the splendid Houelt Cross, HOUELT PREPARAVIT PRO ANIMA RES PATRIS EIUS (Houelt prepared this cross for the soul of his father Res), probably refers to Hywel ap Rhys, who was King of Glywysing and died in 886. The stones suggest that Llanilltud was used as a royal burial ground during the ninth and tenth century. Three miles north of Llantwit Major is the village of Llysworney, the site of the royal court for the cantref of Gorfynydd. The implied association of Llysworney with Llanilltud gave the monastery a high status at least up until the eleventh century, when it was eclipsed by the community at Llancarfan. A number of the charters in the *Liber Landavensis* show land being taken away from Llanilltud in order to diminish its status as part of the successful attempt in the late eleventh century to make Llandaff the episcopal seat of the new diocese rather than Llanilltud – or indeed anywhere else.

Life at Llanilltud

With no specific record, we can only speculate about life at Llanilltud during this period using what we know about other monasteries. Over the six hundred years from the founding of Illtud's monastic school to the coming of the Normans, the buildings in the *llan* would have been extended or rebuilt, as they were originally constructed out of wood, wattle and daub; more was added, and at some point the whole *llan* was relocated further inland, either to be out of sight of Viking raiders following repeated attacks or because of the royal patronage. With gifts and financial support from the royal court, the church, on its new site, may have been embellished. A tall cylindrical pillar with interlaced decoration, generally accepted as dating from the tenth to eleventh century, now in the Galilee Chapel, has a deep 'V' shaped groove cut down the right-hand side from top to bottom, which suggests that it had an architectural function. A fragment of a stone, also now in the Galilee Chapel, is probably the remnant of a matching pillar. The two could have flanked the door of the church, or framed a chancel screen or arch.[169] Malcolm Thurlby has found analogies to the Llanilltud pillars in tenth-century churches in Spain and Norway, where stone pillars support wooden screens.[170] He suggests that a twelfth-century date for the Llanilltud pillars should not be discounted, given the similarities in decoration to pillars from the twelfth-century Herefordshire School of Sculpture. If the pillars are part of a pre-Norman church, it would still have been relatively small, accommodating the altar in a limited sanctuary space and allowing for a modest congregation.

With the need for bibles and liturgical books, it is possible that a library was built – but was there a scriptorium? Llanilltud obviously did not produce Gospel books of the quality of the Lindisfarne Gospels or the Book of Kells, but Gifford Charles-Edwards suggests that the inscriptions on the Houelt Cross and the Samson Pillar cross now in the Galilee Chapel of St Illtud's Church emanate from a milieu with a working scriptorium,[171] with the decorative carvings coming from a monumental mason's workshop with highly-skilled sculptors either at Llanilltud or somewhere else in the area. There are clusters of early medieval carved crosses with similarities to the Llanilltud stones now preserved at Ewenny, Merthyr Mawr and Margam, but these places were not necessarily their original sites. It is also possible that the carved stones were the work of travelling craftsmen.

It was the task of monks to copy and illustrate manuscripts within a scriptorium. The artist of the eighth-century Lindisfarne Gospels was Eadfrith, a Bishop of Lindisfarne; the ninth-century Book of Kells was the work of monks of Iona and Kells; the tenth-century Benedictional of St Aethelwold was illumined by the monk Godeman in Winchester. Every early medieval book that has some inscription of the artist is the work of a monk. However, as Bede shows in his *Ecclesiastical History*, lay craftsmen would be attached to a monastery and allowed to live within the enclosure, some becoming lay brothers and therefore following the pattern of life of the priest-monks. Later, it was commercial craftsmen in travelling workshops who would be employed to build or decorate within the monastery: this was certainly the case post-Norman conquest, as we know from masons' marks and stylistic similarities. An example of a lay workshop is the twelfth-century Herefordshire School of Sculpture[172], which seemed to have travelled from place to place undertaking commissions. Its craftsmen retained local traditions in their work, including Celtic elements, as can be seen at Kilpeck in Herefordshire.

Unfortunately, it will not be possible to prove any theory about the scriptorium and workshops that influenced or produced the carved stones at Llanilltud or the collections now housed in churches nearby. T.M. Charles-Edwards has analysed the inscriptions on the Llanilltud stones, showing that the Latin is not of a good standard.[173] He writes of the eighth-century Samson pillar cross, "The poor quality of the Latin is remarkable given the elevated status of the people concerned and the reputation of Llanilltud Fawr as a place of high Latin culture." His conclusion is that "the intellectual decline at this church between the sixth century and the seventh appears to have been calamitous." By the late ninth century, Old Welsh had influenced the pronunciation and hence the spelling of the Latin inscription on the Houelt Cross, with similarities of spelling on inscriptions on stones at Merthyr Mawr and Margam. "What is striking is the change from the post-Roman period: then Latin was the language of higher status [...] The tools of literacy, spelling included, were primarily those of Latin, only secondarily those of British [...] In this ninth-century inscription, however, Latin was impregnated with Welsh phonology and, even more surprising, Welsh spelling habits".[174] The fact that there seems to have been a decline in intellectual rigour in Llanilltud by this time is clearly illustrated by the inscription on the Houelt Cross where the Second Person of the Trinity is omitted, reading [I]N INOMINE DI PATRIS ET [S]PERETUS SANTDI (In the name of the Father and of the Holy Spirit). This must have been carelessness on the part of the inscriber, perhaps himself illiterate, in copying the text from a wax tablet that was not corrected by his monk overseer; the crudity of the inscription contrasts with the exceptionally fine decoration, obviously the work of a different and more careful sculptor.

The scriptorium at Llanilltud, on this evidence, would not have been of the calibre to produce manuscripts of the quality found in other monastic houses, perhaps partly explaining why none have survived. It would also suggest that by the eighth century, there was no longer a school at Llanilltud teaching the full curriculum recorded by the *Vita Samsonis*. The twelfth-century *Vita Iltuti* only makes passing reference to the school at Llanilltud in the deed from King Meirchion granting Illtud the land: "Your school will be revered, vassals will serve thee and all born in the country. Many will flow together from divers parts, may they be instructed in liberal education."[175] The school at St Cadoc's monastery at Llancarfan had eclipsed that at Llanilltud, with Llancarfan charters listing the eleventh-century *magister* or schoolmaster, Lifris, and the *lector* or reader, Joseph.

Apart from the huts for members of the community, another building within the *llan* would have been the *hospitium* or guest house. With its position near the coast and with easy access from the former Roman roads, Llanilltud would have welcomed many visitors, and so the guest house is likely to have been one of the largest buildings in the *llan*. It would have provided accommodation for those who might wish to join the community, those seeking medical help, and those coming as penitents.

The form of worship at Llanilltud would have developed over the centuries as liturgical books became available for copying, particularly those brought from Ireland. No missal, the order for celebrating the Mass, remains from this period. However, the Stowe Missal, compiled in Ireland in the eighth century, gave instructions for the priest, including the words he would say. It followed the pattern that would have generally been used in the Western Church. As we have seen, up until the eighth century, Llanilltud would have developed its own words and rituals in common with other monasteries in the Celtic lands but, following the acceptance by the Welsh Church of Roman practices in 768, a standardised form would be used. The Mass was celebrated on Sundays and holy days, while the Daily Office of prayers, hymns and psalms remained the weekday pattern of worship.

Although the ecclesiastical status of Llanilltud declined in the centuries leading up to the Norman Conquest, it was probably as a result of its royal patronage that the community acquired, through gifts, land in the Vale of Glamorgan and the Gower Peninsula. This led to disputes as the diocese of Llandaff was being established. The *Liber Landavensis* records "great contention" over land in the Gower between Bishop Oudoceus and Biuon, "Abbot of Illtyd, who said the land was his, the aforesaid land was at last by true judgement, adjudged to St Oudoceus and the Altar of Llandaff."[176] As Oudoceus was Bishop in Glamorgan and Gwent at the end of the sixth century, with no "Altar of Llandaff" at that time, the reference to him was included to bolster the claims of the later diocese.

Members of the community would have had to spend a considerable amount of time in farming: this was the *labora*, the daily work, which all monks would be expected to undertake. However, how much of this would have been the responsibility of lay brothers, or later of hired labourers, is unknown. The growing of wheat for bread, with fields needing to be ploughed and sown and the grain stored, threshed and baked, would have been very labour-intensive. The *Vita Iltuti* mentions three barns in Illtud's time; and that the land was fertile, abounding in harvests, flowing with honey, and fragrant with flowers. The writer compares it to Italy: Llanilltud is more abundant and more temperate, without Italy's excessive heats, so that "the reapers rejoice, more joyful than the reapers of Italy".[177] This of course is a twelfth rather than sixth-century description. The *Vita Iltuti* shows that there were also cattle at Llanilltud, and in passing mentions sheep, livestock essential for milk, meat and clothing. The animal skins would have been used to prepare vellum and parchment as a writing material for the community's books. Fish is also mentioned, as one would expect with Llanilltud's proximity to the sea and rivers.

Spirituality

We are hindered in describing the spirituality of the monks of Llanilltud during this period, as, with perhaps one exception, almost no written material remains. The romantic picture of Celtic Christian spirituality that arose during the eighteenth and nineteenth centuries was that the monks communed with nature, regarding it in an almost animistic way and having absorbed the pre-Celtic religions. Iolo Morganwg suggested that "the Ancient British Christianity was strongly tinctured with Druidism." More critical twentieth-century writers have seen the feeling of God's immanence in his creation in what is described as Celtic Christian spirituality as almost amounting to pantheism, arising out of druidic and bardic traditions. However, while the ancient Celtic traditions were christianised, with the respect for wells, springs, groves and other sacred sites leading to them being given saints' names,[178] it was the Bible – and in particular the Psalms – recited daily, which provided the greatest influence on anything that might be called 'nature spirituality'.

Examples of early Welsh poetry are to be found in The Black Book of Carmarthen, an anthology compiled in about

1250 but containing poems from a much earlier date. Oliver
Davies and Fiona Bowie point out the significance of the
earlier poems in the Welsh context.[179] The convention was for
monks to communicate with other monks in Latin prose: the
various Lives to which we have referred were written in Latin.
However, the ninth- and tenth-century works in The Black
Book of Carmarthen were poems written in Welsh, although
they were composed by monks and are mostly concerned
with monastic life. As we have seen from the Houelt Cross at
Llanilltud, classical Latin was becoming infused with Welsh
spelling conventions. We do not know the provenance of the
early poems, but they could be typical of writings reflecting
the spirituality of the monks of Llanilltud. A tenth to eleventh
century poem in Early Middle Welsh begins:

> Glorious God, all hail.
> May church and chancel bless you,
> may lowland and highland bless you,
> may the three fountains bless you,
> two above the wind, one above the earth;
> may darkness and daylight bless you,
> may satin and fruit-trees bless you.[180]

In another tenth- to eleventh-century Early Middle Welsh poem,
a monk reflects on the month of May with its rhythm of nature
and agriculture as he mourns members of his community, his
'loved ones', who have died:

> Maytime is the nicest time,
> birds are loud,
> trees are green;
> ploughs are in the furrow,
> oxen in the yoke.
> The sea is green,
> lands have many colours.
> When cuckoos sing
> on the tops of fine trees,
> sadness

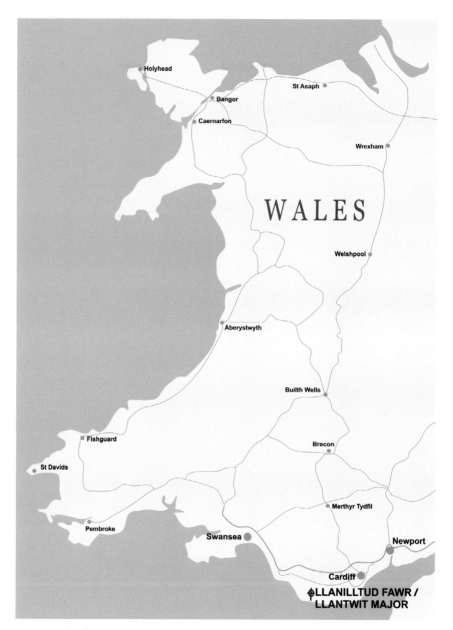

Location of Llanilltud Fawr

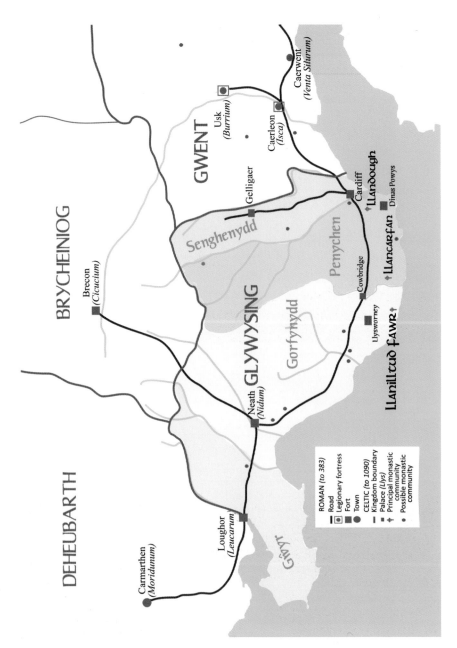

Morgannwg from the Romans to the Normans

DEHEUBARTH

BRYCHEINIOG

GWENT

GLYWYSING

Carmarthen
(Moridunum)

Loughor
(Leucarum)

Neath
(Nidum)

Brecon
(Cicucium)

Gelligaer

Usk
(Burrium)

Caerleon
(Isca)

Caerwent
(Venta Silurum)

Cardiff
Llandough
Dinas Powys

Senghenydd

Penychen

Gorfynydd

Cowbridge

Llancarfan

Llysworney

Llanilltud Fawr

Gŵyr

ROMAN *(to 383)*
Road
Legionary fortress
Fort
Town
CELTIC *(to 1090)*
Kingdom boundary
Palace *(Llys)*
Principal monastic community
Possible monastic community

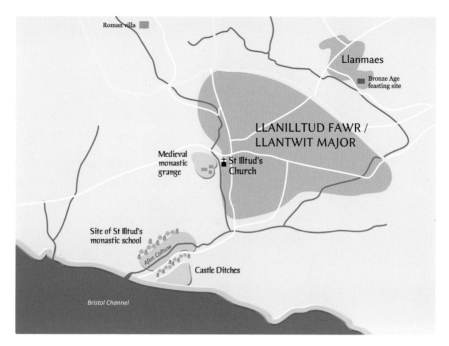

Llanilltud Fawr

Site of St Illtud's monastic school

Castle Ditches and Cwm Colhuw

Llantwit Major beach

Llanilltud Fawr and the Celtic countries

St Illtud's Church, Llantwit Major: Galilee Chapel

Houelt Cross

Houelt Cross: detail of head

Houelt Cross: inscription

Samson or Illtud Cross: inscriptions

Samson or Illtud Cross

Stones from Galilee Chapel Gallery

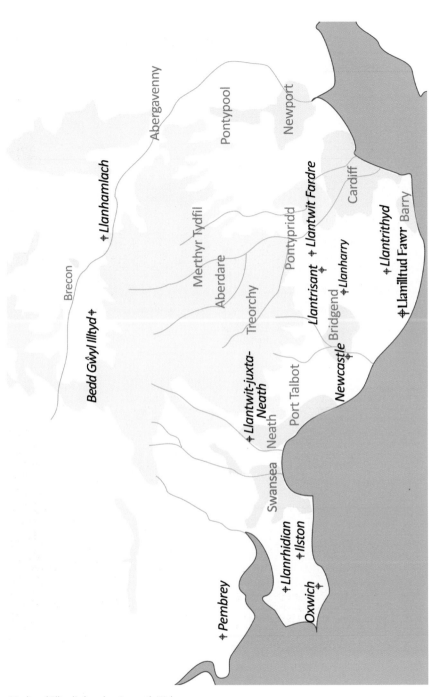

Medieval 'Illtud' churches in south Wales

St Illtud's Church, Llantwit Major, from the south-east

St Illtud's Church from the east

St Illtud's Church

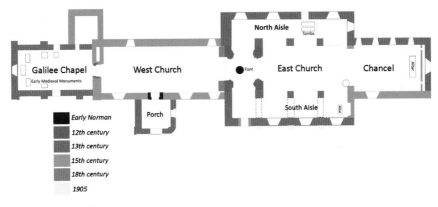

North Aisle
Tombs
Galilee Chapel
Early Medieval Monuments
West Church
Font
East Church
Chancel
Altar
Porch
South Aisle
Altar

Early Norman
12th century
13th century
15th century
18th century
1905

St Illtud's Church: plan

St Illtud's East Church

St Illtud's Church: Jesse Niche
(© Keith Brown)

St Illtud's Church: wall painting of St Mary Magdalene

St Illtud's Church: figure of Jesse

St Illtud's Church from the north-west, showing the restored Galilee Chapel

Galilee Chapel before restoration

Galilee Chapel before restoration

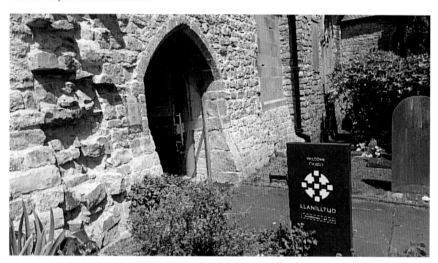

Galilee Chapel entrance

Entrance to Galilee Chapel from West Church

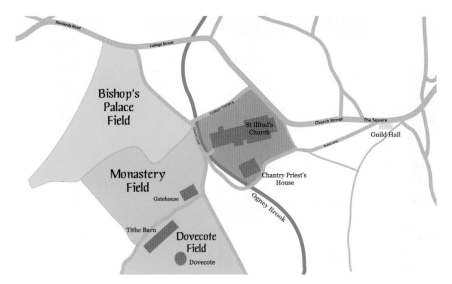

Tewkesbury Abbey's monastic grange at Llanilltud Fawr

Dovecote

Gatehouse

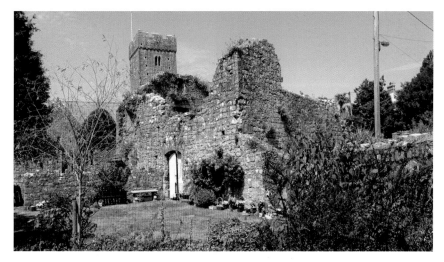

Chantry Priest's House

East Window, St Illtud's Church: stained glass representation of St Illtud with his plough

© Pam Lewis

grows.
Smoke stings,
at night I'm all too restless
since my loved ones
have gone to the grave.[181]

The earliest poem that has been found written in Old Welsh is from the ninth century, a poem of praise to the Trinity contained in the Juvencus manuscript, now in Cambridge University Library. The manuscript was originally produced in Wales as a copy of the text of a fourth-century Latin poem *Evangeliorum Libri IV* (Four Books of the Gospels) by a Spanish Christian, Juvencus. The poem was copied by an Irish scribe, Núadu, who was probably attached to a monastery in south-east Wales. When he completed his work, more than ten different scribes added notes to it, one of whom gave his name in a cryptogram as 'Cymelliauc, a priest'. The only Cymelliauc known from this time is the Abbot of Llanilltud who, as we have seen, is recorded in the Anglo-Saxon Chronicle as Bishop of Archenfield or Ergyng. Earlier, as Abbot of Llanilltud, he received grants from Hywel ap Rhys, the King of Glywysing, who erected the Houelt Cross in memory of his father. The Old Welsh poem was written in the margin – could this have been by Cymelliauc, and composed at Llanilltud? Indeed, could the whole of the Juvencus manuscript have been produced at Llanilltud?

The poem is known as the 'Juvencus nine', as it comprises nine *englynion* or three-line verses:

Almighty Creator, it is you who have made
the land and the sea...
[...]

The world cannot comprehend in song bright and melodious
even though the grass and trees should sing
all your wonders, O true Lord!

The Father created the world by a miracle
it is difficult to express its measure.
Letters cannot contain it, letters cannot comprehend it.

Jesus created for the hosts of Christendom
with miracles when he came
resurrection through his nature.

He who made the wonder of the world,
will save us, has saved us.
It is not too great a toil to praise the Trinity.

Clear and high in the perfect assembly,
Let us praise above the nine grades of angels
the sublime and blessed Trinity.

Purely, humbly, in skilful verse
I should love to give praise to the Trinity,
according to the greatness of his power.

God has required of the host in this world
who are his, that they should at all times
all together fear the Trinity.

The one who has wisdom and dominion above heaven,
below heaven, completely;
It is not too great toil to praise the Son of Mary.[182]

This is a hymn of praise to God's work of creation, so wondrous that even if the grass and the trees could sing – a reference to Isaiah 55:12 – that would be inadequate; even "letters", here meaning the best poetry and prose, cannot fully express the miracle of creation. The poet calls on the Church, as "the perfect assembly", to praise the Trinity, stressing that "it is not too great a toil" to do this.

While there is no written material that can reliably be said to have emanated from the community at Llanilltud, the sculptures may help in an understanding of the spirituality of the monastery. The early medieval Christian monuments now gathered in the restored Galilee Chapel of St Illtud's Church were originally scattered around the churchyard, but were brought into the West Church during late nineteenth-century restorations. Their arrangement along the west wall was not satisfactory, being surrounded in later years by the clutter generated by a vibrant living church; now they can be viewed from all sides as they were originally intended to be.

The late ninth-century Houelt Cross is the only one at Llanilltud to have retained its wheel cross head, though three others now in the Galilee Chapel probably once had similar heads. The Christian Cross, in various forms, is found on stones in Wales dating from the fifth century, the earliest having a simple cross carved on what were perhaps previously Roman milestones and set up as boundary marks. More elaborate crosses were erected within the *llan* around which the Daily Office would be said or sung; later crosses with inscriptions marked the burial places or were the memorial stones of an abbot, such as the Samson Pillar at Llanilltud, or the local royal benefactor, in the case of the Houelt Cross.

The wheel cross surmounting a tall shaft is the most familiar design on early medieval stone sculptures and is found in Ireland, Scotland and Wales. It usually takes the form of a cross without a figure, though decorated with plait work and surrounded by a circle, again usually decorated. It is an integration of the old pagan symbol of the sun, considered in pre-Christian thought to be the divine centre of the cosmos or the 'light of the world', with the Christian symbol of the Cross, the sign of redemption and of the true Light of the world. The circle thus becomes a Christian symbol: a shape with no beginning or end, the Alpha and the Omega, a sign of victory. This iconography of the cosmological cross is not distinctive to the Celtic lands: it can be found in fifth-century mosaics in Ravenna in Italy, for example in the Basilica of Sant' Apollinare in Classe where the Cross floats in the stars; in the writings of the early Church Fathers such as the third-century Irenaeus of Lyon and the fourth-century Gregory of Nyssa; and in the hymns of the sixth-century Bishop Venantius Fortunatus.

The wheel cross began to appear in sculptures in Ireland in the eighth century, at a time when the Irish missionaries were travelling to Italy and returned having seen the images of the Cross in churches there. The ring was developed as a symbol of the cosmos in a form that was suitable for stone carving, resulting in the familiar cross-in-circle that is found, for example, in eighth- to ninth-century crosses at Ahenny (Tipperary) and Kilkieran (Kilkenny), and the St John Cross at Iona, the monastery founded by the Irish missionary Columba on the island off the Scottish coast. In Wales, wheel crosses are generally found in the south, a classic example being Llanilltud's Houelt Cross. Other wheel crosses may be seen in the Margam Stones Museum, gathered from the local area, and possibly carved at the same workshop as Llanilltud's stones.

Of the some four hundred early medieval inscribed stones remaining in Wales, only three have a representation of the crucifixion, with the figure of Christ on the cross. The earliest is at Llangan, six miles north of Llantwit Major, which has been dated on stylistic grounds to the late ninth or tenth centuries. It has to be recognised that carved and inscribed stones have been lost over the years, some used as building material for churches and much figurative sculpture perhaps destroyed at the Reformation or by Oliver Cromwell's soldiers; but the overwhelming representation is of an empty Cross, usually surrounded by a ring. The figure of Christ on the Cross appears on Irish High Crosses, but is not found in Wales.

It has been suggested that the reason why an abstract image should be used on the Welsh crosses, rather than a representation of the Crucifixion as found in Continental art, was that the Pelagian prejudice against representational art still persisted.[183] However, the wheel cross (such as the Houelt Cross) is more likely to reflect the particular spiritual emphasis placed on the Crucifixion in the early Welsh monastic tradition.

The crosses proclaim the victory of the Cross and the joy of the Resurrection, the theme of *Christus Victor* that can be traced back to the early church fathers. It is found in Irish poetry and prayer such as the invocation 'Be Thou My Vision', usually attributed to the sixth-century Irish Christian poet St Dallán Forgaill, though some scholars give an eighth-century date. It concludes with this stanza:

> High King of Heaven, thou heaven's bright Sun,
> O grant me its joys after victory is won;
> Great heart of my own heart, whatever befall,
> Still be thou my vision, O Ruler of all.

Christ won a great victory on the Cross, defeating the powers of evil, and so "death of death and hell's destruction", as the eighteenth-century hymn writer William Williams of Pantycelyn expressed it. The influences of the early Church fathers through people such as Germanus, pilgrims returning from Italy and even from as far afield as the Holy Land, together with the use of liturgical hymns such as those of Bishop Venantius Fortunatus (530–609) proclaiming the victory of the Cross[184] in monasteries such as Llanilltud, would have shaped this particular aspect and understanding of the events on Calvary and led to its expression in the sculpted crosses.

There were probably many more inscribed stones carved at or for Llanilltud over the six hundred years up until 1100 than the four now preserved in the Galilee Chapel. Boundary stones with a simple cross, and the elaborate crosses within the *llan*, would not only remind those seeing them of the message of the Gospel that they represent but would also be places where people would gather for prayer. The monk, when he woke, would look out from his cell and see the Cross:

> The first word I say
> in the morning, when I arise:
> may Christ's Cross be my armour about me.

This is the first of the *englynion* in a poem in The Black Book of Carmarthen: the writer is preparing for a journey and sees the protection of the Cross as a breastplate. The inscribed cross on a stone was also seen as protection, warding evil away from the *llan*, and particularly effective against enemies such as Viking raiders. It was the Christian symbol that was understood by all, educated and illiterate: a talisman, the triumph of good over evil, and therefore the ultimate protection.

It is tempting to look for a symbolic meaning in the distinctive Celtic decorative design on the Houelt Cross and the others at Llanilltud. The interlaced line is endless, representing eternal life. However, the knot pattern and plait work are found in many cultures: for example in the West in Roman mosaics, including those at the Roman villa at Caermead in Llantwit Major. Those gazing upon the interlaced pattern may have found some symbolic significance in it, but the sculptor was using patterns with which he was familiar and could see in secular art.

The Vikings

"The Vikings are coming, the Vikings are coming!" would have been the terrifying cry from the sentry on watch at Castle Ditches above the monastery at Llanilltud as he sighted the many-oared ships coming along the coast. People and cattle would have taken shelter within the earthworks of the fort, providing some defence, but the monastery on the valley floor would have been vulnerable.

The first Viking attacks on Wales took place in the north in 852, with sporadic incursions up until the beginning of the tenth century, when the Vikings concentrated their attention on Ireland. There were fifty years of relative peace until raids from Dublin took place along the Welsh coast – particularly in the south-west, with St Davids being repeatedly attacked. Because of its proximity to the coast, Llanilltud could not avoid attacks by pirates and later by the Vikings sailing up the Bristol

Channel from Ireland. The earliest attack may have been at the end of the eighth century, with occasional raids during the ninth century. The most significant attack was in 988, when the *Brut y Twysigion* records that the monasteries at Llanilltud and Llancarfan were sacked. There were undoubtedly other raids, but there are no written records.

We can only surmise what form the attack on Llanilltud took. The repeated raids on the monastery at St Davids were severe: the buildings were destroyed and monks were killed, including even the Bishop on one occasion. In the raids from Dublin, people were frequently taken back there as slaves. However, there were also some Viking settlements near to Llanilltud, particularly on the islands and immediate coast of the Bristol Channel, as evidenced by Scandinavian names such as Sker, Flat Holm and Steep Holm. Tusker Rock, off the coast near Ogmore-by-Sea, is named after Tuska, a Danish Viking who settled in the area along with his fellow warriors. A few miles from Llanilltud is the village of Wick, a Scandinavian name meaning 'a station for ships', which perhaps became a base for Viking settlement and the launching of raids, but also for trade further up the Bristol Channel.

Why should the Vikings particularly attack monasteries? Not necessarily for the riches they held, in the case of a relatively poor community such as Llanilltud. It was primarily because of Christian attempts to forcibly convert pagans: in 782 the Holy Roman Emperor Charlemagne introduced the death penalty for those refusing baptism and beheaded 4,500 pagan prisoners. This resulted in the Vikings associating Christianity and its symbol, the cross, with violence, terror and subjugation.

Communities such as Llanilltud were considerably weakened as a result of the Viking raids, though it managed to survive until the Normans arrived in the late eleventh century. Local legend has it that the villagers of Llanilltud grew tired of the raids by the Irish and the Vikings and fought back, defeating a band of raiders by enticing them into the village with dancing girls and wine, and then attacking them. The villagers celebrated their victory annually on 3 May, the date of the battle, during a festival which was known as *Diwrnod Anwyl Llanilltud*, Llantwit's Bold Day.

5

LLANILLCUÔ ANÔ ThE NORMAN CONQUESC

1066 and all that

The final chapter of the twelfth-century *Vita Iltuti* is an eyewitness account of what would seem to be an actual event occurring at Llanilltud, which must have taken place between 1088 and 1107. It describes the attack by the native Welsh and the defensive use of Castle Ditches by the inhabitants of Llanilltud. The opening sentences of the chapter set the historical context:

> When William, King of the English, was reigning throughout Britain, and Prince Robert Fitzhamon was ruling Glamorgan, the Northern Britons began zealously to resist the King, and afterwards in common and firm confederacy with them the Southern Britons. They wasted and burnt villages and towns. The foe came from the woods to injure their English-born and Norman-born fellow-countrymen. They laid waste and returned to distant mountains and to woods with immense plunder. In the meantime an army was put in motion by the Welsh of about three thousand armed horsemen and footsoldiers to waste and burn Glamorgan.[185]

The William is William Rufus, the second son of William the Conqueror, who succeeded to the throne of England following the death of his father in 1087. Robert Fitzhamon, born in

Normandy in 1045, was granted the barony of Gloucester following his support for William Rufus during a rebellion in 1088, and eventually became Lord of Glamorgan. He was severely injured in battle at Falaise, Normandy, in 1105, and died two years later.

The earliest reference to the Normans in Morgannwg after the Battle of Hastings in the *Brut y Tywysogion* – the primary source for the medieval history of Wales, written in the twelfth century – is Caradog ap Gruffudd's seizure of the kingdom with the help of Norman soldiers in 1072; the condition for this help was that he became a vassal of King William I (the Conqueror). Caradog was deposed in 1081 by Rhys ap Tewdwr, Prince of Deheubarth, who came to a financial arrangement with William in order to rule the kingdoms of south Wales. In the same year, William made a pilgrimage through south Wales to St Davids. It was not his intention to conquer Wales but to ensure that the border between England and Wales was secure, to prevent incursions into English territory by rebellious Welsh princes. However, the Norman lords began pushing into Wales, especially after William died, because unlike his father, William Rufus gave them free rein. As each piece of territory was gained, a motte and bailey castle was built, soon to be replaced by a more substantial stone castle. The Welsh were almost defenceless against the well organised and well armoured Norman knights.

Robert Fitzhamon soon expanded from his barony of Gloucester to take Glamorgan from Rhys ap Tewdwr, though exactly how and when is not recorded in contemporary documents. The legend of the Twelve Knights, written about by Sir Edward Stradling of St Donats in 1561, says that Robert Fitzhamon defeated Rhys ap Tewdwr in battle in 1090 and then he and his knights took possession of Glamorgan from his base at Cardiff Castle. Fitzhamon divided the land up into lordships or manors for his knights, giving each the responsibility of subduing and controlling the native Welsh in his lordship;

Fitzhamon retained for himself the fertile Vale of Glamorgan, the Kingdom of Glywysing. However, it was only the coastal plain of Glamorgan, including the Vale, which effectively came under the control of the Normans; the Welsh princes continued to have power over the *blaenau* or uplands and made frequent raids on the Norman-controlled areas. It was one of these attacks that is recorded in the *Vita Iltuti*. Whether or not it was an exaggeration to say that three thousand Welsh attacked Llanilltud, it made a good story to say that the Welsh were defeated by a smaller number, including "unarmed women" and "weak boys". The account in the *Vita Iltuti* shows that by this time the community of Llanilltud had placed itself – or had been placed – firmly under the patronage of the Normans and enjoyed their protection.

More raids by the Welsh princes on the lowlands of Glamorgan took place throughout the twelfth century, particularly following the death of King Henry I in 1135, when a period of civil war known as the Anarchy began that lasted until 1153. However, there is no record of Llanilltud being attacked. During the rule of William Fitzrobert, 2nd Earl of Gloucester from 1141 to 1183, there were clashes with the Welsh. On his death, there was a major revolt throughout south Wales, but again no evidence of Llanilltud being involved.

Llanilltud and the Diocese of Llandaff

In 1092, Robert Fitzhamon founded the Benedictine Abbey of St Mary in Tewkesbury, on the site of a tenth-century Benedictine priory. In a charter of 1106, it is recorded that King Henry I confirmed "to the Church of Tewkesbury these things written below, which Robert Fitzhamon and many other men have given, or which Abbot Gerald has bought, namely [...] the church of Llantwit."[186]

The fortunes of the community at Llanilltud declined after the Viking raids in the late tenth and early eleventh centuries, with Llancarfan becoming the most powerful monastic community in Glamorgan. As we have seen, there does not seem to have been a monastic school at Llanilltud since the eighth century, and unlike at Llancarfan, there is no written record of one at Llanilltud immediately prior to the Norman Conquest. Charters list some of the eleventh-century members of the *clas* at Llancarfan – the Abbot, the *magister*, the *medicus* and the *lector* – but no such list remains for Llanilltud. What is presented in one section of the *Vita Iltuti* as a description of life in the monastery in St Illtud's time is probably that of the community or *clas* prior to the Norman Conquest, as it contains so many anachronisms:

> ....and being appointed Abbot, the venerable man [Illtud] appointed fifty Canons, who at suitable times and fixed hours visited the church, having each of them his prebend, to wit, each his own homestead with profits, which were given by the people to keep in memory their souls. Yearly rents were paid to the Abbot; what was paid he divided by commot custom.[187]

The writer has used Norman terms, Canon and prebend, to describe the pattern of life as he would have understood it at Llanilltud prior to the community coming under the control of Tewkesbury Abbey: the clerics, priests or monks lived in their own homes but gathered together throughout the day in the church for the Divine Office, under the rule of the abbot. It was probably an exaggeration to say that there were 50 members of the *clas* at Llanilltud at that time: the *Vita Cadoci* claims only 36 Canons for Llancarfan[188] but the reality is that at both there were very few.

When the Normans arrived in Wales, they discovered a Church that, although it saw itself as part of the wider Western Catholic Church, was not under the control of Canterbury. They also found that there was no centralised structure: that although there were bishops exercising episcopal oversight within an area, these were either abbots of monasteries or attached to them rather than administering a diocese with a *cathedra* or seat in a cathedral. In order to have complete rule in the territories they had conquered, the Normans realised they had to radically change the old Welsh ecclesiastical order. The first stage was to disband the old *llannau* and transfer the monasteries and their possessions to the English or Norman Benedictine foundations. So it was that Robert Fitzhamon gave the church of Llantwit and all its possessions to Tewkesbury Abbey; the Abbey would appoint the Canons for what would become the Collegiate Church of St Illtud. He gave a monastic farm of 158 acres of land to the west of the church to the Abbey, which became known as West Llantwit or Abbot's Llantwit; but he retained the best land, the cornfields of Llanilltud, which became a rich granary for his garrison at Cardiff.

The second stage was to establish the dioceses. A diocese of Llandaff was beginning to emerge during the years immediately preceding the Norman Conquest, when the body of St Teilo was reputed to have been removed from Llandeilo Fawr in Carmarthenshire to the church at Llandaff. A bishop called Joseph was styled 'Bishop of Teilo', but was based at Llandaff between 1022 and 1045, resulting in an episcopal area stretching from the River Wye to the River Tywi and encompassing Gwent, Glamorgan and much of Dyfed. Joseph's successor Herewald attempted to consolidate the diocese, but was based at Ergyng in the east rather than at Llandaff. It was Urban, appointed bishop in 1107, who was the first who could rightly be called Bishop of Llandaff. Urban was the first Welsh bishop to swear canonical obedience to the Archbishop of Canterbury. He played a full part in the life of the province of Canterbury, attending consecrations of bishops and Church councils. He began the building of a cathedral at Llandaff, close to the Normans' administrative centre in Glamorgan, and subsequently the name Llandaff was used for the title of the diocese.

In order to have rights as Bishop of Llandaff and an episcopal manor to provide income, Urban would have to relinquish any claim to church lands under the control of Robert Fitzroy, 1st Earl of Gloucester. This he attempted to resist, even though he needed the Earl's patronage. There was also resentment that churches and lands should be given to an abbey such as Tewkesbury or Gloucester, outside the diocese. In addition, Urban was losing the land to the west of Glamorgan and to the east of Gwent to the Bishops of St Davids and Hereford respectively, with the result that the boundaries of the diocese of Llandaff were becoming established as those of the old kingdoms of Glamorgan and Gwent. So in order to establish himself and the diocese of Llandaff, Bishop Urban had to fight a battle on two fronts, against the Norman lords and his neighbouring bishops – and seemed to be losing.

It is in this context that the *Liber Landavensis* was compiled in about 1120, with other documents added later. It contains the Lives of Dubricius, Teilo and Oudoceus, who it regards as the first three Bishops of Llandaff; an abridged version of the *Vita Samsonis;* papal bulls; and numerous charters which were intended to show that grants of land were made to the diocese by various kings from the sixth to the eleventh centuries. This was the evidence that Bishop Urban was using to prove his claim to land within the diocese, but more importantly to show that the diocese of Llandaff was the most ancient in the country and could be traced back to Dubricius, claimed to be its first archbishop. This is why a Life of St Samson is included, in order to show that it was Dubricius who consecrated bishops and who therefore held metropolitical status in western Britain, rather than an Archbishop of St Davids. The Life also shows that St Samson was a disciple of St Illtud and subsequently Abbot of Llanilltud, the monastery "founded by St Germanus", which was necessary to prove his orthodoxy and therefore that of Dubricius.

The documents within the *Liber Landavensis* to a large extent rewrote the past to justify the present. While they should not be completely dismissed as forgeries, they represent the vision Bishop Urban had of the history, status, possessions and boundaries of the diocese of Llandaff. They give a twelfth-century picture of the diocese, rather than of anything from the time before. Similarly, it is for this reason that we have to constantly remind ourselves that the *Vita Iltuti*, which was written at about the same time, contains little of historical value apart from the last chapter. It shows that it was Dubricius who appointed Illtud and marked out the *llan* of Llanilltud, and therefore that the monastery was under the control of the diocese – and should still be so, in the view of the bishop – rather than the abbey of Tewkesbury.

When Bishop Urban went to Rome in 1128 to prove his case, it is not clear whether he used the documents in the *Liber Landavensis* as evidence. The dispute with the Norman lords over some of the lands and tithes mentioned in the *Liber Landavensis* was settled in the diocese's favour in various papal privileges, but more land was conceded to the Norman lords. In 1126 Bishop Urban had made an agreement with Robert Fitzroy, Earl of Gloucester, "concerning all the claims which that bishop had against the aforesaid earl and his men in Wales, and concerning those lands which they did not acknowledge to hold from the bishop".[189] The bishop gained the manor of Llandaff, a mill, wood, and fishing rights, but "on account of the aforesaid things which the earl grants and yields to the bishop, the bishop dismisses and quit-claims to the earl all claims which he had against him and his men concerning all those lands which they avow to the earl's fee." The dispute over the appropriation of churches and land by English abbeys was settled as far as Tewkesbury was concerned in a charter drawn up by Urban's successor, Uchtred:

> The Charter of Uchtred, Bishop of Llandaff, made to Roger, Abbot of Tewkesbury, and to the Convent at the intervention and with the consent of Robert, Earl of Gloucester, in AD 1146, concerning the controversy which was between the aforesaid Bishop, and Abbot, and Monks, about tithes and other things, namely, concerning

the claim which the same Bishop had brought against them concerning the same, the contents of which are as follows: the same Bishop concedes to God and the Church of the Blessed Mary of Tewkesbury and the monks, to have and to hold, peacefully and quietly, all the tithes, alms and benefices which have been given to them in that Diocese, or hereafter shall be given canonically...[190]

This sealed the position of Llantwit Major, which was confirmed in subsequent charters such as that of 1180:

The Charter of Nicholas, Bishop of Llandaff, confirming to the Church of Saint Mary of Tewkesbury, and the monks, all the Churches and their benefices with their belongings which they have in that Diocese by the bounty of Christ's Faithful, namely [...] the Church of Llantwit with the Chapel of Lisworney.[191]

The ancient connection between Llantwit Major and the *llys* (court) of the kings of Glywysing at Llysworney was being maintained, the chapel there later being rebuilt as the present St Tydfil's Church.

The reference to churches and benefices in the charters illustrate how by the end of the twelfth century the parochial structure was established in the new diocese of Llandaff. There was only one archdeacon covering the whole of the diocese, which was divided into six rural deaneries: three in the Gwent part of the diocese and two in the Glamorgan part. Llantwit Major fell in the Groneath rural deanery, which stretched westward from the River Thaw. From the 1180 charter onwards, we have seen that the parish of Llantwit Major included Llysworney, which it retained until the nineteenth century. Nicholas of Llysworney was the Dean of Groneath in 1246, suggesting that by then Llysworney had its own priest, though it remained part of the parish of Llantwit Major.

Once the organisational structure of the diocese was to a large extent sorted, with a cathedral being built at Llandaff, the Normans had to deal with some of the practices of the old Welsh Church to bring it in line with Rome. By placing the old *clasau* of Llanilltud and other Welsh monastic communities under the control of English abbeys, the Normans ensured that they would follow the Benedictine rule and also be under the episcopal oversight of the Bishop of Llandaff. The 1180 charter lists the other churches in the diocese that had been given to Tewkesbury, and states that Bishop Nicholas "concedes also, that on the cession of the rectors of these [churches], the monks may establish in them fully qualified vicars, that is, in priests' orders, who are to be answerable to the Bishop for spiritualia (a proper sustenance being assigned to them), but who are to hand over to their [the monks'] use all other possessions of these [Churches] in tithes as well as in lands".[192] The old system of hereditary appointment was replaced by one of patronage by the bishop, abbey or lord of the manor; when appointed by the lord of the manor, the priest was styled 'rector', but when by the bishop or abbey, he was styled 'vicar'. As we will see, in the special case of Llanilltud, in the thirteenth century the Abbey, as lord of the manor, appointed a rector to lead the college of monks, while the bishop appointed a vicar for the local congregation.

The Normans also had to deal with the question of clerical celibacy. Councils convened by various popes throughout the eleventh century banned clerical marriage and forbade clergy to live with any women, including their wives, implying that the practice of married clergy was widespread. The First Lateran Council, held in 1123, decreed that the marriages of all higher clerics were invalid; and the Second Lateran Council of 1139 banned married men from being ordained. In the light of the papal prohibitions on clerical marriage, the writer of the *Vita Iltuti* felt it necessary, as part of the process of establishing the diocese of Llandaff, to show the conformity and credibility of St Illtud because of his connection with Dubricius, and therefore concocted the story of Illtud sending his wife Trynihid away before taking monastic vows and subsequently being ordained. However, despite these papal orders, according to the *Brut y*

Tywysogion, Urban's successor as Bishop of Llandaff, Uchtryd, was married, with a daughter and a son who was a monk of Gloucester.[193] We must presume that Bishop Uchtryd was not the only cleric who was married with a family at that time.

The building of St Illtud's Church

There is no contemporary documentary evidence to help us construct the story of the building of St Illtud's Church. From the reference to the "church of Llantwit" in the 1106 charter we must assume that a stone church had been built by that time, either on the site of the later monastery or on what would have then been a new site. All that remains of the first stone church is the unembellished round-headed south door into the present West Church of St Illtud's Church, the font with its scallop decoration, and the foundations of the walls. Excavations during restorations at the beginning of the twentieth century showed that the Norman church was cruciform, with north and south transepts and a chancel, stretching about 28 feet into the present East Church.[194] If Thurlby's dating of the two grooved pillars now in the Galilee Chapel as belonging to the early twelfth century is correct,[195] they could have formed part of a screen between the crossing of the transepts and the chancel; or if they are of an earlier date, they could have been re-used from the pre-Norman church. The Norman church remained as both the collegiate church for the Canons of Llantwit Major and the parish church for nearly one hundred and fifty years.

The Cult of St Illtud

Honouring the memory of saints, venerating them as miracle-workers, appealing to them as intercessors, devotion to their relics, and pilgrimages to saints' burial places and shrines – these were practical aspects of the cults that built up around the memory of particular saints. Lives of the saints would be written, often many centuries after their death and with little basis in fact. Churches or *llannau* dedicated to a particular

114

saint would be established, on a site which it was claimed had been visited by the saint. This phenomenon, of course, was not peculiar to the saints of the Church in the Celtic lands but was the pattern throughout Christendom, reaching its height in later medieval times with many undertaking pilgrimages across Europe, to Rome and the Holy Land.

Evidence of a cult of St Illtud can be found in the string of churches dedicated to him in south Wales and in Brittany. However, there was no particular shrine of St Illtud, and indeed no historical evidence of his burial place, though a local tradition claimed it to be on Mynydd Illtyd in the Brecon Beacons, near to the present Brecon Beacons National Park Visitor Centre. A Bronze Age earth ring is known as *Bedd Gŵyl Illtud*, the Grave of Illtud's Watch, from the practice of keeping a vigil there during the night before 6 November, at the site of his supposed burial. A church dedicated to St Illtud once stood nearby, but was demolished in the 1990s.

Another church dedicated to St Illtud within the Brecon Beacons National Park is at Llanhamlach, east of Brecon. Gerald of Wales, in his *Journey through Wales*, wrote:

> It appears from ancient yet authentic records kept in these parts that while Saint Illtyd was living as a hermit at Llanhamlach, the mare which used to carry his provisions to him became gravid after being covered by a stag, and gave birth to a creature which could run very fast, its front part being like that of a horse and its haunches resembling those of a deer.[196]

There is no mention of this in the *Vita Iltuti*, but the fact that it was a tradition at Llanhamlach that Illtud spent time there as a hermit shows how his cult spread. The "authentic records" could be, as Doble suggests, a lost Life that was read in the church, which is now dedicated to St Peter and St Illtud. To the east of the church is a chambered cairn comprised of three wall stones and a sloping capstone, called Tŷ Elltud on Ordnance Survey maps. On several of the slabs forming the chamber there are incised crosses – some plain, some enclosed in lozenges and some doubled – dating to medieval times. The cairn, which would originally have been completely enclosed, could have provided shelter for a hermit; and the crosses may have been incised by later pilgrims, believing it to be a place where Illtud stayed.

No positive identification can be made of places mentioned in the twelfth-century *Vita Iltuti*, though the local tradition of three churches of probable twelfth-century origin dedicated to St Illtud could be those referred to in the *Vita Iltuti*. One story is of two robbers who stole St Illtud's herd of swine from the sty where they were kept and drove them into woodland. However, they lost their way, wandered round in circles, and ended back at the sty. The robbers made another attempt to drive the pigs, this time up into the hills, but with the same result. "But the heavenly King and supreme Corrector, seeing that those evil doers would not return from their ill-will, changed their bodies into two stones [...] This memorable miracle is credited by posterity, for even till now there is seen the place of the sty, which is called by Illtud's name. Till now too are seen the immovable stones called by the name 'Two Robbers'".[197] The Latin word used for sty is *hara*; the church of Llanharry near Pontyclun is dedicated to St Illtud and was granted in 1180 to Tewkesbury Abbey, so was therefore served by the Canons of Llantwit Major. However, there is no evidence of the 'immovable stones' remaining there today.

As we have seen, the *Vita Iltuti* tells the story of Illtud hiding in the cave near the River Ewenny. Although the cave has not been identified, near to the river is the church of St Illtud in Newcastle, Bridgend. This is listed along with the church of Llantwit Major in the 1106 grant to Tewkesbury Abbey, though its dedication appears as St Leonard in the 1180 Charter. It is not clear when it reverted to St Illtud.

The third church is St Illtud's in Llantrithyd. Although the church is dedicated to her husband, the name of the *llan* is a corruption of Trynihid, presumably so named as a result of the story in the *Vita Iltuti* as the place where "she built a dwelling, she founded an oratory, where most faithfully she prayed to the Lord Redeemer".[198] However, this church is not mentioned in the twelfth-century charters, the earliest reference being in 1254, when it belonged to the manor of Leige, held by the Welsh family of Madoc ap Iestyn.

Other Glamorgan churches dedicated to St Illtud are those of Llantrisant, also dedicated to Saints Gwynno and Tyfodwg, traditionally pupils at Llanilltud, which was also first mentioned in 1254 and given in 1348 to Tewkesbury; Llantwit Fardre, one of the chapelries of Llantrisant, mentioned in 1291; and Llantwit-juxta-Neath. Local tradition says that Illtud came to a small hermitage by the River Neath for Lenten observances, on which site is built the present medieval church.

There is a group of churches on the Gower Peninsula dedicated to St Illtud at Iltson, Oxwich and Llanrhidian. According to the *Liber Landavensis*, the monastery of Llanilltud owned land and property in the Gower, which would account for churches dedicated to St Illtud.

The name Iltson is contracted from Iltwitston, named in John Marius Wilson's *Imperial Gazetteer of England and Wales* (1870–72) as Llanilltyd, with the earliest written record of the church in a charter of 1119. In 1221 the church was granted to the Jerusalem Order of Knights Hospitaller, who then built the present stone church.

The local tradition is that the twelfth-century chancel of St Illtud's Church in Oxwich is built on the site of a sixth-century cell, and that St Illtud brought the Sutton stone font with him when he came to the cave of Llwynarth for three years in order to escape the crowds flocking to Llanilltud. The story of Llwynarth cave is found in the *Vita Iltuti*, abridged from an earlier account in the *Historia Brittonum* by Nennius, written about 828, but with additions that date to after the eleventh century. The *Vita Iltuti* tells of a "marvel in Guyr: an altar miraculously suspended in the air, which is in the place that is called Loyngarth." Illtud was praying in a cave, the mouth of which faced the sea, when a ship steered by two men sailed towards him, carrying the body of a holy man with an altar suspended over his face. Illtud and the men buried the holy man, the altar not moving from its position; the men left, leaving Illtud to build a church around the body and the altar, "and the altar continues to be miraculously suspended there unto this very day".[199] It is not known who the 'holy man' was, as Illtud was sworn to secrecy, but the description by Nennius of the site of the cave and the church fits the situation of St Illtud's Church, Oxwich.

The thirteenth-century church at Llanrhidian, built by the Knights Hospitaller, is dedicated to St Rhydian and St Illtud. It has been suggested that Rhydian is a corruption of Trynihid, Illtud's wife, or was otherwise a pupil of Illtud. In the parish was the holy well of St Illtud, an account of which appears in the *Annals of Margam* in 1185, when:

> in the district known as Gower, in the *villa* called Landridian, on Wednesday, there was a copious flow of milk, lasting for three hours, from a certain fountain, which the inhabitants of the place called the Fountain of S. Iltut. Several persons who were there state that they saw with wonder the well continue to pour forth milk, while butter was forming on the edge of the spring.[200]

There are two other ancient church dedications to St Illtud in Wales. St Illtud's Church, Pembrey, in Carmarthenshire, was granted in 1120 to the Benedictines of Sherborne Abbey by the Lord of Kidwelly. A reference in the *Liber Landavensis* may suggest that it once belonged to the monastery of Llanilltud, as one of the priests is listed as 'Gurhi, son of Silli, the *doctor* [or teacher] of Lanniltut'. Another connection may be through the le Botiler family, who had a manor in the village in the twelfth century and whose crest can be seen in the church. Their main estate was that of Dunraven, Southerndown, six miles along the coast from Llantwit Major; an incised slab with a life-sized figure in full armour of Sir John le Botiler, who died in 1285, lies under the altar of St Bridget's Church, St Brides Major. However, another John le Botiler, born about 1264, was from Llantwit Major. He was part of the household of Maurice of Berkeley in 1312 and became cupbearer to Hugh Despenser the Younger in 1322, the last of King Edward II's favourites and ruler of south Wales until 1326. In 1324 John le Botiler became MP for Gloucester and is recorded as such until 1339. The fifteenth-century oak roof of the West Church of St Illtud's, Llantwit Major, contains a boss of the le Botiler family.

The Church of St Illtud, Llanelltyd, in Merionethshire, stands within a circular graveyard which is believed to date back to pre-Norman times. The present church is late fifteenth century but originated in the twelfth century, with some stones remaining from that date.

With the exception of Llantwit Major, none of the churches dedicated to St Illtud in Wales or the sites on which they stand can be definitively dated to before the Norman Conquest through either documentary or archaeological evidence. However, a few are set within non-rectangular graveyards which could be pre-Norman: Llanhamlach, Llanharry, Llantrisant, Llantwit Fardre, Llantwit-juxta-Neath, Oxwich and Llanelltyd. It is early medieval inscribed stones which provide us with possible evidence of the existence of pre-Norman churches.

The earliest incised cross in a church dedicated to Illtud is at Llantrisant, which has been dated to the seventh to ninth century.[201] A similar cross was found near Llantwit-juxta-Neath, again dated between the seventh and ninth century.[202] A stone incised with a 'cartwheel' cross was found set in the boundary wall of the churchyard at Llantwit-juxta-Neath, and has been dated to the late tenth- to eleventh-century. The two most fascinating pre-Norman stones are at Llanrhidian and Llanhamlach, as both include carved figures. The Llanrhidian stone is a massive limestone slab with incised patterns. On the face is what appears to be a lion's head and two human figures flanked by dog-like animals. The human figures follow the style found on Irish high crosses and manuscripts, and it has been suggested that they represent St Brigid and St Patrick. It is not clear what the stone was used for; perhaps as an architectural feature in the same way that the pillars at Llanilltud were used, or as the base of a font. It is dated to the ninth to tenth century,[203] though Thurlby characteristically suggests it could be from the early twelfth century, based on parallels for the composition elsewhere.[204] The stone at Llanhamlach has been dated to the tenth to eleventh century and probably stood within the circular *llan*. It has an incised cross flanked by a male figure holding a book, together with a female figure: presumably St John holding his Gospel and Our Lady. One of the inscriptions reads [-I]OHANNIS *[The cross] of John*, the other records that Moridic erected the stone.[205]

The dedication of churches cannot be relied upon to show an early cult of a saint, but may only have been given as the result of a Life being written and circulated hundreds of years after the saint's death. A number of the churches dedicated to Illtud were built on what would seem to be pre-Norman sites, but may only have received their dedication as the result of the *Vita Iltuti* and the attempts by Bishop Urban within the diocese of Llandaff to claim a historical line back to St Dubricius through St Illtud. Some have legends of St Illtud attached to them, but those are of late origin and do not necessarily reflect his movements. The dedication of a church to St Illtud is more likely to be the result of land in the area being owned by Llanilltud in its immediate pre- or post-Norman state than of a cult of St Illtud in the traditional sense of devotion to him.

While we cannot be certain that a cult of St Illtud existed outside of Llanilltud prior to the Norman Conquest, the references to Illtud as a soldier in the *Vita Cadoci* and the *Vita Iltuti* gave rise, as we have seen, to the popular tradition of *Illtud Farchog*, Illtud the Knight, and would thus have given impetus to the development of a cult around the soldier-saint. *Illtud Farchog* would have appealed to the Normans as a fellow-soldier, or even as a knight of the Round Table, a true warrior just like them; and so even though they preferred their own saints from the Roman calendar, such as the apostles and the Virgin Mary, they were ready to accept dedications of the churches to him. But in so doing, the native Welsh also found encouragement and support in St Illtud in fighting for their freedom from oppression by their English overlords, and ultimately for their independence. When Edward Lhuyd visited north Wales in 1699 as part of his grand tour through Wales, Ireland, Scotland, Cornwall and Brittany to gather information for his *Archaeologia Britannica*, he says that he discovered that the people of Llanelltud in Merionethshire knew nothing about their patron saint, Illtud, other than that he was *"Elldyd Farchog"*.

As we have seen, because of the association of St Illtud with St Samson, the founder of the diocese of Dol, and with St Paul Aurelian, the founder of the diocese of Léon, there are a number of churches dedicated to St Illtud in Brittany, although there is no historical evidence that he travelled there. Lanildut and Locildut retain his name. The parish church of Coadout is dedicated to St Illtud, as was the parish church of Troguéry, and there are chapels of Sant-Illtut in the parishes of Saint-Pabu and Plouguiel. *Pardons* are still held in honour of St Illtud on 6 November in Brittany.

Llanilltud from the Thirteenth Century to the Reformation

The extension of St Illtud's Church

Despite the continuing conflict in the thirteenth century between the Welsh princes and the English lords, this was a time of relative peace and prosperity for Llantwit Major. Its manor was held securely by the lords of Glamorgan, allowing for the church to be extended to a size out of proportion to the small population of the community. The transepts and chancel of the Norman church were levelled and replaced by a new nave of four bays with aisles and a chancel. A low tower was erected over the division between the Norman church – known as the Old Church or West Church – and the New Church or East Church, and a large porch was added to the West Church. The porch incorporated a room above it, now called the Parvise Room, which may have been used as a schoolroom, as in some other churches. In addition, a chapel was added to the west end of the church, now called the Galilee Chapel. This had a lower storey, which formed a crypt with a processional passage through it, an upper half-storey with an altar, a piscina for washing the sacred vessels used for the Mass, and a niche formed out of the previous west window of the West Church.

Why was the church effectively in three parts? Traditionally the West Church has been regarded as the parish church for Llantwit Major and the East Church as the monastic church for monks from Tewkesbury Abbey. However, there is no documentary evidence to show this. The only reference to the use of any part of the thirteenth-century church is in the *Annals of Tewkesbury Abbey* of 1230, which states that the Abbot of Tewskesbury "retained a certain chapel adjoining the said Church in token of our possession." Did a monastery or a college continue at Llanilltud until the Reformation in the sixteenth century? We will return to this question later.

Further work took place in the fourteenth century. The south aisle had extended to the full length of the chancel, but this was shortened to balance the north aisle, which was the length only of the nave. This meant that the south wall of the chancel had to be rebuilt, and a chancel arch with squints erected. In the fifteenth century, the West Church and the Galilee Chapel were rebuilt with an Irish bog-oak roof that ran through the two, and a two-storey building called the Sacristy was joined onto the north side of the West Church and the Galilee Chapel. The east window of the chancel was inserted during this time, though the stained glass within it is early twentieth century.

When each of the sections of the church was built, the interior walls would have been highly decorated with a rich and vivid display of figurative art and patterns, in a manner almost unimaginable today as we look at white lime-washed walls. However, some of the wall paintings survive, the earliest being that of St Mary Magdalene on the north wall of the chancel, from the late thirteenth century. She is wearing a red gown and a flowing headdress and holding her jar of precious ointment in her right hand. Just further east on the north chancel wall is an almost indistinguishable figure of a female, probably of the Virgin Mary, again from the thirteenth century.

On the north wall of the nave is a large wall painting of St Christopher – regarded as the patron saint of travellers from the third century onwards – with cloak and staff, carrying the infant Christ through swirling water. This illustrates the legend that St Christopher, from Asia Minor (now Turkey), used to help people across a river, and that one day he carried a child who on the other side revealed himself to be Christ. The wall painting, older than the clerestory window which cuts into it, has been dated as early fifteenth century, the period in which the popularity of the saint reached its height.

Painted above the chancel arch is a chequered pattern set within a frame of circles, forming the background to the former rood screen and now to a rood (erected in 1959), showing Christ on the cross with the Virgin Mary and St John. Surmounting the pattern is a faint painting of the cross with the crown of thorns, the nails, scourge and spear, the symbols of the passion. Patches of decoration can be seen on the nave pillars and in other parts of the East Church, and there is some lozenge patterning in the West Church.

Not in its original position but from the thirteenth-century church is what has been described as "an outstanding piece of early thirteenth-century sculpture".[206] This is the Jesse Niche, which is now on the east wall of the south aisle of the nave, but may originally have been part of a reredos for the early thirteenth-century church or have been in the western chapel, now the Galilee Chapel. It is a carved stone representation of the ancestry of Christ as recorded in St Matthew's and St Luke's Gospels. At the base is Jesse, the father of David, lying asleep. Out of his side grows a tree, the branches climbing and twisting as a vine on either side of the niche. Within the branches are the fourteen crowned heads of the kings of Judah of the house of David, rising to the head of Christ at the top. It illustrates Isaiah 11:1: "A shoot shall come out from the stock of Jesse, and a branch shall grow out of his roots." Traces of paint and gilding can be seen, as the whole thing would have been painted. A carving of the Virgin and Child probably stood within the niche. In 1858 the figure of Jesse is recorded as being in a niche in the Galilee Chapel, but the branches on either side of the niche were in their present position in the south aisle. The architect G.E. Halliday, who was responsible for the restoration of St Illtud's from 1900 to 1905, believed the base with the figure of Jesse was placed in the Galilee Chapel when the rest of the niche was moved from the original thirteenth-century reredos to the south aisle in the fourteenth century. He reunited the figure of Jesse with its branches.

Behind the altar of the East Church is an elaborate stone reredos, carved in the late fourteenth century and set a few feet from the east wall to provide space for a priest's vestry, which was entered through two doors on either side. The twenty-two niches, of varying sizes, would each have contained a statuette of a saint. During the restoration in 1899 a statuette of the Virgin and Child was discovered, though this seems too small to have been one of the originals from the reredos; this is now in one of the south aisle windows. The upper part of the reredos was largely reconstructed in the 1905 restoration.

The College of Llantwit Major

The road to St Donats that runs along the east side of the churchyard is called College Street, and that on the north side is College Gardens. These names reflect the local tradition that, at least in medieval times, there was some sort of educational establishment run by the monks of Tewkesbury near to the church. Unfortunately this has been confused with the original monastic school of St Illtud, probably as a result of Iolo Morganwg claiming that the field to the north of the church was its site. The field was marked on the 1877 and 1897 Ordnance Survey maps as "Côr Tewdws *(site of)*", the College of Tewdws. Tewdws or Theodosius was the Roman Emperor from 379 to 395, who Iolo Morganwwg claimed had founded Llanilltud. Various excavations were made but nothing pre-

Norman was discovered. The final excavations were made in 1937 by V.E. Nash Williams of the National Museum of Wales in Cardiff, but he had to conclude that no excavation has "yielded any evidence bearing on the problem of the pre-Norman occupation of Llantwit Major".[207]

The *Annals of Tewkesbury* make no mention of monks being resident at Llantwit Major, of a college or school there, or of the building of the church in the thirteenth and fourteenth century, despite the amount of money that this would have entailed. However, as we have seen from Nicholas, Bishop of Llandaff's charter of 1180, Tewkesbury Abbey was required to appoint a vicar, who was answerable to the Bishop. This it did during the first half of the thirteenth century, endowing the vicarage with all the altar-dues, the great and small tithes, and the tithes of the chapel of Llysworney.[208] In 1254, a valuation for taxation purposes mentions a rectory valued at £2 per annum, and a vicarage at £5. In 1291, the rectory is assigned to the Abbot of Tewkesbury, with the vicarage valued separately.

This suggests that during the thirteenth century there were two priests for St Illtud's, one appointed by the Bishop of Llandaff and one by the Abbot of Tewkesbury, which may also account for the division of the church into 'west' and 'east', the former perhaps for the parishioners of Llantwit Major and the latter for the use of Tewkesbury Abbey. A similar division took place at nearby Ewenny Priory, where the western nave was used as the parish church, and the eastern presbytery was kept for the priory, a daughter house of St Peter's Abbey in Gloucester.

The size and splendour of the East Church of St Illtud's suggests that it was regarded as necessary to provide for a good number of monks, although there is no record of them. The designation could have been of a college of monks; it was certainly not a priory as at Ewenny. According to the architect John Rodger, who was involved in the restoration of St Illtud's Church in 1905, local tradition says that the door on the north side of the East Church was placed there "for the convenience of the priests, whose residence was on that side of the church on the site of the present Council Schools. This residence was at a higher level than the church, and tradition says that it was reached by flights of stone steps."[209] Rodger also refers to Plymouth House to the north of the church, "stated traditionally to be one of seven halls or hostels for the residence of students in medieval times".[210] This no doubt arose out of the claim by Iolo Morganwg that Illtud founded seven churches, appointing seven 'companies' for each church and seven halls or colleges in each company, with seven saints in each hall or college.

In the Revd Dr David Nichols' *The Antiquities of Lantwit Major,* compiled in 1729, he writes of Llantwit's school or college:

> We do not find any mention of the time when it became extinct, but we may well think that it remained until the Reformation, for there was a School, of time out of mind, then at Lantwit for educating youth in Latin learning and logic that was maintained by a portion of the Church profits and by the Abbot's rents that were sold to one of my ancestors, and in whose family they still remain. When these rents and other incomes of tithes and pasture were sold, the school ceased, to the loss of the place.[211]

The school may not have been directly run by monks of Tewkesbury Abbey, and so there is no mention of it in the *Annals of Tewkesbury* or any medieval valuation document.

The Monastic buildings

The Ordnance Survey maps of 1877 and 1897 designate the field to the west of St Illtud's Church as "Monastery *(site of)*" and the field to the north of that is marked "Bishop's Palace *(remains of)*". There is no evidence of there ever having been a bishop's palace at Llantwit Major, so that designation is curious, again probably based on local tradition without any basis in fact. However, two thirteenth-century buildings, the gatehouse and dovecot, still stand to the south-west of the church; and it is known that surviving into the nineteenth century there was a tithe barn, clearly marked on the 1879 Ordnance Survey map. The excavations by V.E. Nash-Williams in 1937 in the supposed 'monastery field' revealed a long narrow building which could have been an ox-house or stable, and another building which could have been a farmhouse, leading him to conclude that there was an extensive complex of medieval buildings, "typical of the planning of a medieval monastic grange".[212]

As we have seen, in the early twelfth century Robert Fitzhamon gave the land to the west and north of St Illtud's Church to Tewkesbury Abbey. By the thirteenth century, this was being worked from a grange occupying the 'Bishop's Palace field', the 'monastery field', and the field in which the dovecot stands, its boundary being marked by an embankment. In addition to the gatehouse, the dovecote (which would have provided eggs and meat), and the now-lost large tithe-barn, the excavations show that the grange probably included a dairy, storehouses, a brewery, ox-house, stables and accommodation for the labourers.

The grange was probably leased to lay tenants at an early date, providing a secure source of income for the abbey. There is an interesting little story in the *Annals of Tewkesbury* from 1230. William, the parson of the "Church of Llandirwit", was long in dispute with Peter, the Abbot of Tewkesbury, as he wished for his brother to take on the tenancy of the grange "by hereditary right as is the custom with the Welsh." The abbey allowed the brother to farm the manor of Llantwit for eleven marks yearly, but "if the said farmer shall not pay his rent, he shall lose it for ever".[213] In the Ministers' Accounts for Tewkesbury Abbey for 1449, William Dedy of Aven is named as the lessee of "the farm of the site of the Rectory of Lantwyt with buildings and columbary built on it, and 5 closes of land".[214] The accounts mention the "ox house of the manor", a granary, a cottage and a water mill. In 1535, the Abbey, in return for the tithes, supplied the parishioners of St Illtud's with a bushel of corn to make the sacramental bread.

The fortunes of the manor of West Llantwit or 'Abbot's Llantwit' suffered during the fourteenth century as a result of the Black Death of 1349, and also because of weather conditions. A contemporary account states that "by reason of the drought of the weather", grass did not grow in the fifteenth year of King Richard II (1392), with the result that the corn crop failed and famine ensued. Then in 1402, Owain Glyndwr and his rebel Welsh army swept through Gwent and Glamorgan, targeting the English institutions and anglicised communities. The monastic foundations particularly suffered, including Ewenny Priory and Llandaff Cathedral, with the Bishop's palace left in ruins. Llantwit Major, seen as an 'English' town, was attacked, with half the inhabitants fleeing, the original town hall and other buildings burnt to the ground, and the crops of the manor of Boverton and Llantwit Major – 'the granary of the Vale' – destroyed. Surprisingly, however, the manor of West Llantwit was not attacked, even though it belonged to an English abbey; and St Illtud's Church and the grange buildings were left untouched.

The Raglan Chantry

The final development of St Illtud's Church before the Reformation was the rebuilding of the Norman West Church and of the western chapel. With its two storeys, and used exclusively by the monks of Tewkesbury Abbey, the chapel served as the Lady Chapel and as the 'Galilee', where the procession formed to enter the main church for Mass, recalling that it was in Galilee that Christ commenced his ministry. Stairs led from the eastern end of the crypt or Galilee to the Lady Chapel, this upper storey covering half of the chapel to the processional doors on the south and north side.

Some time before the end of the fifteenth century or the beginning of the sixteenth, the chapel was endowed and adapted to become a Chantry Chapel for the benefit of the Raglan family. An additional gallery was inserted at the western end, which could have been for a choir or as the lord's loft for the Raglan family to use during the Mass.

The first of the family was Robert ap Jevan. Following the death of his father in 1418, he went at the age of 10 to live with his uncle, Sir William ap Thomas, at Raglan Castle in Monmouthshire, and assumed the surname Raglan. In 1445, Robert was granted land to the north of Llantwit Major as payment for his work as steward to the Earl of Warwick in the manor of Boverton and Llantwit Major, having previously married Joan Clarke, the daughter of William Clarke of Knoyles Place, Llantwit Major, while he was working there. With the income from the land they built a new house, suitable for a steward, in the centre of the town. This is now the Swan Inn, just up from St Illtud's Church.

The chantry was established by Robert and Joan's sixth son, Sir Hugh Raglan, Vicar General to the Bishop of Llandaff. According to a document drawing on information provided by Sir Hugh's great-nephew in 1572, this was "for all christien sowles in the west end of the church of lantwitt, and [he] bought certeyn Lands in his lyff tyme, which afterwad he gave unto certynbe feffes[215] [...] to the use of finding of a chantery prist which daily should pray for his Sowle and all christen sowles in the said chappell."[216] The preference was that, if any "kyndsmen of the name of Raglan were a prist", he should be the stipendiary chantry priest. This came true, as Edmond Raglan, one of the family of Robert Raglan, received 27s. 5d. as "priest of Our Lady's Service". The chantry owned a chalice worth 51s. 4d. and a pair of old velvet vestments worth two shillings. However, somewhat confusingly, a priest was also appointed for the chantry, holding the office of 'priest of Our Lady's Chantry' in perpetuity and receiving £5 18s. 2d.

The chantry priest lived in a house on the south side of the churchyard, the walls of which are still standing. When chantries were abolished between 1545 and 1547, the Chantry Priest's House became a private dwelling, and was most recently a smithy until it was hit by a bomb in 1940. In addition to saying Mass daily for the souls of members of the Raglan family, the priest's duties also included providing hospitality for visitors.

The Chantry Chapel itself eventually fell into a roofless ruin, shown as such in an engraving of 1829, until it was rebuilt in 2012–2013, primarily to house the early medieval monuments.

The Reformation

The Reformation in the diocese of Llandaff affected the English-founded monastic houses such as Ewenny, Margam and Neath, all of which were shades of their former selves by the sixteenth century, with very few monks left. However, the more important issue facing the Welsh people at the time was the radical changes that were taking place in the political landscape. As a result of the Laws in Wales Acts of 1535, commonly called the Acts of Union, Wales became a full and equal part of the kingdom of England. The old lordships were fused together to form shires; the County of Glamorganshire was formed from the twelve tribal areas of the *Blaenau* or uplands, the six boroughs of the Vale and coast plain, and the lordship of Glamorgan. Wales was brought under English law, old local Welsh customs were suppressed, and those using the Welsh language were prevented from taking public office. The Reformation was seen in this context, as part of English legislation and the imposition of the English faith.

The requirement of all clergy to assent was the first stage of the changes following the Act of Supremacy of 1534, by which King Henry VIII became Supreme Head of the Church of England – and in Wales as a result of the Laws in Wales Acts. It would seem that all the clergy in the diocese of Llandaff did so. It is interesting that it was a Grey Friar of Cardiff, Henry Bureman, who signed the assent as chantry priest of

Llysworney in the parish of Llantwit Major.[217] The second stage was a survey of all church property, to assess their value in order to transfer payments hitherto made to monastic houses to the Crown. In January 1535, a Commission consisting of the bishop, justices of the peace, agents of the Crown and local gentry was appointed for the diocese of Llandaff, to list the names of all who held office, details of all the property, and their whole and yearly values, including revenues, pensions and fees. On completion, the Commission's work had to be passed to the King's Exchequer, to be included in the *Valor Ecclesiasticus* (church valuation). The living of Llantwit Major was classified in the *Valor* as a vicarage worth £16, but it was noted that Tewkesbury Abbey drew some tithes and other receipts.

In November 1535, on the completion of the *Valor* for Llandaff, two Crown visitors began a visitation of the diocese. In April 1536 they completed their work to determine how monastic patronage and property should be dealt with. Tewkesbury Abbey was dissolved in 1536, so the patronage of Llantwit Major passed to the Crown, who in turn passed it to its Dean and Chapter on the creation of Gloucester Cathedral in 1540. The Abbot's Llantwit was sold to Sir Thomas Stradling of St Donats in 1543 for £183 13s. 9d., though the Grange buildings were retained by Gloucester Cathedral.

The next stage was the suppression of the chantries, or more specifically the appropriation of the endowments that had been made to provide chantry priests. In 1548 a new Commission consisting of laymen was formed to survey the chantries in the diocese. At Llantwit Major the salaried priest of Our Lady's Service was removed as a result, but because the priest of Our Lady's Chantry held his post in perpetuity, he was not. The churchwardens were responsible for procuring pensions for dispossessed priests; Edward Raglan, the priest of Our Lady's Service, received £1 7s. 5d per annum. In their report, the Commissioners also listed the number of communicants in the towns of the diocese; Llantwit Major had 360. The Chantry Chapel and the Chantry Priest's House were bought by James Turberville of Llantwit Major.

The final act was the confiscation of church goods, which took place between 1552 and 1553. King Henry VIII had died in 1547 and was succeeded by Edward VI. Owing to the new king's need of money and aware that he had contracted terminal tuberculosis, commissioners were sent into every parish to confiscate as much as possible before the young king died. From St Illtud's, the commissioners appropriated four chasubles, one cope, one altar frontal, one red velvet suit, eleven candlesticks, and other easily transportable goods. We can only but imagine the despair of the parish priest and parishioners of St Illtud's and other churches in the diocese as they were left with little other than their building. A petition was sent in 1554 from the diocese to the Lord Chancellor of England under the new Queen, Mary, which said "that, whereas in the latter days of King Edward VI, a commission was directed to certain gentlemen in Glamorganshire for the sale of Church goods, those Commissioners have detained in their own hands the most part of their goods [...] Further [...] that they had not made any restitution to the parishes, in spite of the fact that they had received many letters from the Queen's most honourable Council to that effect."[218] As a result, in 1555, four local men were asked by the Crown to examine the process of the confiscation of church goods, and they did so by visiting every church in the diocese and meeting with the clergy and wardens. They submitted their report in 1556, but although they were able to show that the commissioners had indeed kept the confiscated goods for themselves, nothing was done; and with the death of Queen Mary in 1558 and the accession of Queen Elizabeth I, the Reformation was re-established. The Church was impoverished, the diocese of Llandaff was without a bishop for a number of years, the Cathedral was in a poor state of repair, and the clergy were demoralised.

For Llantwit Major, the Reformation meant that over a thousand years of monasticism or connection with a monastery had ended. St Illtud's Church was no longer a collegiate church but a parish church served by a vicar, who, until the disestablishment of the Church in Wales in 1920, when it ceased to be part of the Church of England, was appointed by the Dean and Chapter of Gloucester Cathedral.

Keeping the Memory of Llanilltud Alive

Seventeenth to Twenty-First Century

The Revd Dr David Nichols

The Nichols were the most prominent landed gentry of the area, living first in the Great House, High Street, in Llantwit Major, then in Ham Manor, which was demolished in the 1960s. The Revd Dr David Nichols was vicar of Llantwit Major from 1660 until 1720. He reportedly wrote *The Antiquities of Lantwit Major*, a copy of which was lent to Iolo Morganwg, who gave it to David Williams to be included in his book *The History of Monmouthshire* (1796), along with a number of other appendices which he supplied. It must be accepted that there is a possibility that Iolo Morganwg may have actually written *The Antiquities of Lantwit Major* himself; but if it is indeed genuine, it is one of the earliest extant histories of Llanilltud – though still not to be relied on.

Nichols had access to the *Liber Landavensis*, in which, he says, "we find many accounts of the Abbots of Lantwit and of the school founded there by St Iltutus. It was the University, we may call it, of Britain during its continuance, which was till the time of the Norman conquest." He records that the school had "came to naught in the time of Henry the Eighth" but "that when it became poor and little, was not much talked of or noticed by historiographers, it being so much below the great schools and universities that were at that time in England".

Perhaps it is to Nichols that we can attribute the claim that Llanilltud was the earliest centre of learning in Britain, for he writes "The most learned Writers agree, that St Iltutus founded his school and monastery about the year of our Lord 450 [...] and this was the first school of learning in Britain; some will have it to be the first Christian school in the world; but that is not true; suffice it to be the first in Britain. [...] The ruins of the school of St Iltutus are to be seen at this day behind the church hard-by; and the university halls and buildings stood in a small field west of the school, where some ruins are still appearing."

Nichols used the *Liber Landavensis* and the *Vita Iltuti* to construct his history of Llanilltud, but made some interesting additions. He claimed that his family was descended from Illtud, giving that name to the eldest son. He says that at St Illtud's school at Llantwit "were more than two thousand students and holy men, and where all the sons of Kings and Nobles, whether in Britain or Bretany, were educated [...] An old MS. of Sir Edward Stradling's (of St Donats) says that the Saints of Lantwit monastery had for their habitation four hundred houses and seven halls, which must mean, I guess, that they lived in separate houses like the common little dwellings there still remaining, and that they had seven large buildings for assembly, which were like our halls, or we may deem them colleges." Ignoring the numbers, it is interesting that the description of Llanilltud is accurate in respect of Celtic Christian monasteries. Stradling's manuscript recognised that the monks lived in separate dwellings, with some communal buildings.

John Wesley

John Wesley, the Anglican clergyman who was one of the three founders of Methodism, made a number of journeys through south Wales, preaching in churches or people's homes. In his diary for Friday 25 July 1777 he recorded his visit to Llantwit Major:

> About 11, I read prayers and preached in Llantwit Major church to a very numerous congregation. I have not seen either so large or so handsome a church since I left England. It was sixty yards long, but one end of it is now in ruins. I suppose it has been abundantly the most beautiful as well as the most spacious church in Wales.

The ruin was presumably the Galilee Chapel.

Iolo Morganwg

The stonemason Edward Williams (1747–1826) is better known by his bardic name Iolo Morganwg. He has been described as an architect of the Welsh nation, whose concern was to preserve the literature and culture of Wales and create a sense of pride in its history. He was a poet, an antiquarian, a political radical and a humanitarian; a colourful character who created the Gorsedd of Bards, which is an integral part of the National Eisteddfod of Wales today. Born near Llancarfan and living in Flemingston for most of his life, Iolo called the Vale of Glamorgan "the paradise of Britain's land". He was fascinated with Llantwit Major because of its history (as he understood it), in particular because of St Illtud's Church, on which he worked as a stonemason. He claims to have discovered many ancient artefacts there, including the Samson Cross.

Iolo's son, Taliesin, collected together and translated his father's papers, which he had proposed as "materials for a new history of Wales". Iolo has been regarded as everything between a hopeless romantic to a historical forger, but we have to accept that he was interpreting the material that was available to him at the time with the aim of presenting the history of Wales to a wider audience than had hitherto been able to access it. However, there are flights of imagination in Iolo's writings. He claims that it was Eurgain, the daughter of Caradog, "who first introduced the faith among the Cambro-Britons" in 55 AD "and sent for Ilid (a native of the land of Israel) from Rome to Britain. This Ilid is called, in the service of his commemoration, St Joseph of Arimathea. He became the principal teacher of Christianity to the Cambro-Britons, and introduced good order into the choir of Eurgain, which she had established for twelve saints near the place now called Llantwit [...] After this arrangement Ilid went to Ynys Afallon in the Summer Country,[219] where he died and was buried; and Ina, king of that country, raised a large church over his grave, at the place called now Glastonbury."[220]

If pilgrims had thought that St Joseph of Arimathea had visited Llanilltud centuries before and introduced 'good order' there, this would have ensured the fortunes of the town as the Welsh Glastonbury. However, Iolo states elsewhere that it was the Roman emperor Theodosius or Tewdws who had founded Llanilltud, not as a monastery "but rather an enfranchised school, to exhibit and teach the distinguished knowledge and exalted sciences that were known in Rome, and to the Romans at Caerleon upon Usk".[221]

A little later in his genealogy of the kings of Glamorgan, Iolo claims that Tewdric, "an eminently good king", founded many churches and colleges, built the church at Llandaff, and:

> also gave property to the College of Iltutus; and instituted there
> four fair establishments for the votaries of religion and learning.
> It was at his suggestion that this Iltutus brought St Germanus
> to Cambria; for the college of Eurgain was now extinct, having
> been entirely destroyed by the Saxons; but a new, and contiguous
> one was established by Iltutus, through the gifts and affection of
> Tewdric; so that it became the principal college of all Britain, and
> the first in the world for learning and piety.[222]

Typically, Iolo is confused with dates and chronology, as Germanus of course predated Illtud. While here he says that Illtud brought Germanus to Wales and Llanilltud, later he says that Germanus placed Illtud as principal of the College.[223] Tewdric, according to the *Liber Landavensis*, was the King of Gwent and Glywysing killed in a battle at Tintern with the Saxons around the year 630, over a century later than Illtud. Iolo gives the names of the parents of Illtud: "Illtyd Varchog, the son of Bicanus, cousin of Emyr Llydaw; his mother was Gweryl, the daughter of Tewdrig, king of Morganwg, and he was placed as principal of the college, which the Emperor Theodosius founded in Caerworgorn."[224] Bicanus is given as Illtud's father in the *Vita Iltuti*, but not Gweryl as his mother.

Another claim that Iolo makes was that St Patrick studied at Llanilltud, but that:

> the Irish [...] invaded and oppressed Britain; and one of their ships entered the Severn, her crew landed, and seized an immense booty in corn, cattle, and every other moveable property that they could lay their hands upon – among which were included sons and daughters. They also took away Saint Patrick from the College of Theodosius (College of Iltutus) to Ireland; whence that College became destitute of a principal and teacher for more than forty years, and fell into dilapidation; its walls and enclosure being also broken down.[225]

Iolo lists other supposed saints of Llanilltud, some of whom are commemorated in dedications in Glamorgan and Gwent – Ederyn (Llanederyn), Tathan (St Athan, Llanvaches), and Crallo (Coychurch).[226]

As we have seen, Iolo states a number of times that there were two thousand saints at Llanilltud, residing in "eight score and eight halls or colleges", but also that there were seven churches, with "seven companies for each church, and seven halls or colleges in each company, and seven saints in each hall or college", which he computes to be 2,401 persons. The number seven in the Christian tradition is seen as the number of completeness and perfection, which explains why Iolo would want to use it in his description of Llanilltud. "And prayer and praise were kept up, without ceasing, day and night, by twelve saints, men of learning of each company".[227]

While we can be rightly sceptical about Iolo Morganwg and his somewhat confused history of Llanilltud, we can be grateful to him for recovering the Samson Pillar, now in the Galilee Chapel. He tells how, when he was about twelve or fourteen years of age and "fond of history and antiquities", "a very old man", Richard Punter from Llanmaes, who "though only a shoemaker, was a more intelligent person than most of his class", showed him a spot on the "east side of the porch of the old church, at Llantwit, where, he said, a large monumental stone lay buried in the ground, with an inscription on it to the memory of two kings".[228] The local tradition was that it had slipped into the grave of a young Llantwit man, Will the Giant, who at seventeen years of age was seven feet seven inches high. In the summer of 1789, Iolo dug in search of the stone, found it, cleared the earth away, and with assistance from men returning from the fields at harvest, raised it out of the grave. Underneath the stone, he discovered bones of a larger size than usual. The stone lay on the ground nearby until 28 August 1793, when Iolo had help to erect it against the east side of the porch.

Iolo was "satisfied" that the inscription on the pillar, "the Cross of the Saviour that Abbot Samson prepared for his soul, and the soul of King Iuthahel, and of Artmali and Tecan", refers to Abbot Samson, who was "Bishop of Dole, in Brittany, in the sixth century and also Abbot of Lantwit"; King Ithail, "King of Brittany, the contemporary and patron of Samson"; and also to King Artmali, who he was "not able to identify, but think it possible that he, also, may have been of Dole".[229] He based his conclusions on his interpretation of the chronology of persons mentioned in the *Liber Landavensis* and on the work of two historians of the seventeenth and eighteenth centuries, Edward Stillingfleet and Thomas Carte.[230] However, on stylistic grounds and linguistic interpretation, Redknap and Lewis believe the pillar is unlikely to be older than late eighth century.[231] Identifying the names on the pillar has proved problematic. While the Abbot Samson of the inscription seems to appear among the witnesses to various charters in the *Vita Cadoci* and the *Liber Landavensis* from the second half of the eighth century, which would confirm the late eighth century date, identifying the kings has not been so easy. A King Iuthail of Gwent was killed in battle in 848, but the name Iudhail appears in the charter of *c*.765 as *Rege Rotri filio Judhail* (King Rhodri, son of Ithael). The Artmali on the pillar should read Artmail, appearing as such on a stone at Ogmore and elsewhere. He could be the Arthuail mentioned in a number of charters in the *Liber Landavensis*. Tecan could be Teican, a clerical witness in the *Liber Landavensis*. Brian Davies, using the work of P.C. Bartrum from 1948, argues for an earlier date for the pillar, basing his theory on Batrum's chronology of the *Liber Landavensis* charters in which he identifies Samson and the kings as belonging to the seventh century. Davies concludes, "If Peter Bartrum is correct [...] then we have in the church at Llantwit the oldest dateable inscribed standing Christian monument in the British Isles. Thanks to Iolo!"[232] Even accepting the later date, we still have to thank Iolo Morganwg, not only for the discovery of the Samson Pillar but also for his careful record of the Llantwit stones, in order to ensure that their historical value would be respected by later generations. He was concerned about the condition not just of the Llantwit stones but those in other places, asking that people should not break off parts of stones "for whetting their scythes".[233]

Benjamin Heath Malkin

The late eighteenth century saw the rise of cultural tourism, with travellers writing detailed descriptions of what they saw on their journeys, often illustrated by romanticised sketches or paintings. Benjamin Heath Malkin was born in London in 1769, educated at Harrow and Trinity College, Cambridge, and became headmaster of the grammar school at Bury St Edmund's in 1809. In 1830 he was appointed Professor of History in the University of London. He married Charlotte Williams, the daughter of the headmaster of Cowbridge Grammar School, in 1793 at Holy Cross Church in Cowbridge, and died in 1842. A commemoration plaque to Benjamin and Charlotte Malkin can be seen in Holy Cross Church. Malkin was no doubt acquainted with Iolo Morganwg through his association with Cowbridge, and acquired an interest in Welsh history and literature.

In 1803 Malkin made two excursions through south Wales, and the following year published his book *The Scenery, Antiquities and Biography of South Wales* from the material he collected, along with views "drawn on the spot". In his description of Llantwit Major, which it would seem was influenced by Iolo Morganwg, he describes the founding of the community at Llanilltud:

> Illtyd, son of Bocanus, a Breton, accompanied the saints Germanus and Lupus into Britain, on a mission from Pope Celestine, for the purpose of suppressing the Pelagian heresy, as we are commanded to term it on the authority of the church, about the year 430. The first measure they adopted was to establish schools of learning, in which the British clergy might be properly educated. The two first and principal schools were those of Dubric and of Illtyd, both disciples of St Germanus, who appointed the latter head or superintendent of Theodosius's college or congregation, so called because it had been founded by the emperor of that name"[234]

Malkin states that the school "or college [...] patronized by the King of Glamorgan, was at this place, henceforth called after the name of Illtyd, Llantwit, signifying by contraction the church of St Illtyd, with the addition of Major, to distinguish it from other places in the county of Glamorgan also bearing his name."

Malkin credits St Samson with the two crosses that bear the name. Following Illtud's death, he tells us, Samson "took upon himself the superintendence of the school, and erected a monumental cross to his teacher in the churchyard behind the church, as appears by the inscription on its shaft [...] He also erected the large monumental cross, with the circular top lost, standing against the east side of the porch belonging to the old church, as we are likewise informed by the inscription on its shaft."

According to Malkin, in 860 "the Saxon pagans demolished all the monasteries and churches in Glamorgan, and among them the monastery or college of Illtyd." In 959, the college is said to have been destroyed by Owen, son of Hywel Dda; then in 975 and again in 987 by the Danes; and in 993 by Eneon, the son of Owen. Malkin describes the Norman invasion of Glamorgan and the restoration or founding again of the college of Illtyd by Robert, Earl of Gloucester, in 1111.

> This is the last mention of Llantwit, or the college or monastery of Illtyd, hitherto found in the old Welsh histories. But in the ancient register of Llandaff, a copy of which is in the British Museum, and another in Jesus College library at Oxford, there are the names of the Abbots successively, and I believe the whole of them uninterruptedly from Illtyd down to the commencement of the twelfth century, or perhaps lower. This manuscript is in Latin.

Malkin mistakes the medieval grange buildings to be those of Illtud's monastery:

> Near the church some ruinous walls of the school or college founded by Illtyd are still remaining; and they are sufficiently indicated to be of such high antiquity by the circular and segment arches, in the true Roman style, to be seen to this day [...] The gateway to the monastery is still standing, converted into a cottage, with a granary over it for the use of the tithe-barn, which stands near.

143

Archaeologia Cambrensis and the Cambrian Archaeological Association

Malkin mentions "a cross in the same style as that to the memory of Illtyd, lying flat on the ground before the church door, with part of the circular top broken off, and the letters seemingly defaced." This presumably refers to the Houelt Cross, but all the stones are fortunate to have survived, for when members of the Cambrian Archaeological Association visited St Illtud's Church in 1849, they were appalled to learn that "ancient tombstones" were being destroyed. "It will scarcely be believed that, when at Llantwit, I found this fine monument [the Houelt Cross] used for a bench, on which a stone-mason was chipping a modern grave-stone," wrote Thomas Wakeman.[235] The Association managed to halt the destruction, for it was recorded in the minutes of the Annual General Meeting:

> It gives us great satisfaction to state that, in consequence of the energetic representations made by Lord Adare, Mr. Archdeacon Williams, Mr. Bruce Pryce, and other gentlemen, members of the Cambrian Archaeological Association, the destruction of the ancient tombstones, &c, at Llantwit Major has been stayed. We are given to understand that the parochial authorities have become aware of the serious mistake they were on the point of committing, not, however, before one, if not two, sculptured stones had been broken up.[236]

George Petrie, an Irish antiquary who was present at that visit, wrote to the vicar of Llantwit Major that members of the Association had "observed a large monumental slab presenting a sculptured cross of an interesting character and very early date being broken up into pieces at the west door, one half of it cut into square blocks for building purposes, and the other grooved by a mason for a similar operation".[237]

Archaeologia Cambrensis, the journal of the influential Cambrian Archaeological Association, included two articles on St Illtud's Church in its edition of January 1858. The first

144

was by the English historian Edward Augustus Freeman, who described the series of buildings at Llantwit Major as "one of the most striking in the kingdom [...] All around are scattered remains of an earlier antiquity, crosses, memorial and sepulchral, witnesses of the fame of Llantwit in a day so remote that the mediaeval architects regarded its remains as mere materials for their own erections."[238] Freeman was perplexed by the "extraordinary erection at the extreme west end. This had puzzled both myself and every one in whose company I had visited the church, and we had all been inclined to set it down as a portion of the domestic buildings of the monastery." However, he was enlightened by the English archaeologist J.H. Parker, who saw this now roofless building as "a Galilee, or large western porch, with a chapel over it, probably dedicated to St Michael, as was customary for chapels in this situation. It had ascending and descending staircases, one in each corner, at the extreme west end. This was usual, on account of the number of worshippers on particular occasions, when the relics were exhibited in this upper chapel."[239]

The Welsh archaeologist Harry Longueville Jones, writing in the same edition of *Archaeologia Cambrensis*, speculated as to why the Lady Chapel should have been built at the western end of the church, and not at the eastern end beyond the chancel as in many cathedrals and abbey churches. His conclusion was that:

in the case of Llantwit, the difficulty of the ground – rocky and rising steeply behind the chancel – may have suggested the construction of a western chapel, as a more economical plan than the cutting away of the rock at the eastern end. The thought no doubt did not exist before the thirteenth century, because Lady Chapels at east ends of churches only date from that period; and as the existing buildings had been placed so far eastward that an extension of them in that direction would have been difficult, a prolongation of the western end, though anomalous, and possibly inconvenient, was probably preferred.[240]

145

The articles in *Archaeologia Cambrensis* would have aroused interest in St Illtud's and the history of Llanilltud. The January 1849 edition gives an account of a talk by Thomas Wakeman on the Houelt Cross and Samson Pillar: he dates the latter to the middle of the ninth century, contradicting Iolo Morganwg's assertion that it is the sixth-century Samson to which the inscription refers. The Dean of Llandaff, William Conybeare, speaking at the Annual General Meeting of the Cambrian Archaeological Association in 1849, exhorted members to visit Llantwit Major:

> The venerable remains of Llantwit, the earliest college of literary and Christian instruction in south Wales, dating from the sixth century, deserve attention from still higher motives: it would command the same feeling which Dr. Johnson so eloquently expressed on his visit to Iona.[241]

By 1879, the Houelt Cross, which was in two pieces, and the cross shaft were inside the West Church, propped up against the north wall; but the Samson Cross and Pillar and the cylindrical pillars were still in the churchyard.

A description of St Illtud's Church written just before 1888 says that the West Church was "a sepulchre, a charnel [...] a gruesome place indeed." However, in that year the first restoration took place under the direction of the architect G.F. Lambert, when a temporary floor was laid in the West Church to replace one of beaten earth. The rest of the early medieval stones, with the exception of the Samson Cross, were brought into the West Church in 1896.

Alfred Fryer

In 1892, Alfred Fryer, a member of the Council of the British Archaeological Association and Fellow of the Royal Historical Society, gave a lecture to the Association on *Llantwit Major: A Fifth-Century University*, which was subsequently published in book form. He recounted the history of Llanilltud using material from the various Lives of St Illtud and St Samson and the Welsh Triads, and acknowledged the writings of Iolo Morganwg. Fryer concluded his lecture:

> Scholars and bards, historians and poets, zealous missionaries and dignified ecclesiastics received their education at Llantwit; and we may venture to say that when barbarism was not yet extinct, when civil feuds were frequent, when passions were rife, when heresies beset the faithful, Llantwit exercised a wonderful influence, civilizing and teaching the people of Britain and Armorica [Brittany].[242]

In his book, Fryer imagines a student of Llanilltud "clad in his *cuculla* made of wool", giving a guided tour of the University town – with "no domes or towers like our Oxford and Cambridge" – and talking of daily life there and the subjects he studied. Fryer relies heavily on Iolo Morganwg for information on the number and use of buildings at Llanilltud, but elaborates in his description, using information from the seventh-century Adomnán of Iona's Life of St Columba. What he gives us is a description of a seventh-century Celtic Christian monastery such as that on Lindisfarne or Iona. In a limited form this may be applicable to Llanilltud: the church, "with few architectural pretensions"; the refectory, equipped with "ladles and strainers, drinking-cups, knives, and wide but shallow spoons for eating the national dish of porridge"; and a thatched-roofed house which was "nothing more or less than the Bodleian of Bangor Illtyd", with its copies of the books of the Bible, ecclesiastical writers and "profane authors". The imaginary student shows his hut, constructed of wattle and daub, "simple and humble", asking, "What would one of our gay undergraduates of Trinity, Cambridge, or Baliol [*sic*], Oxford, think of such apartments?" The only furniture was a straw pallet bed and a wooden box. The student possessed a rolled scroll of the Psalms, but also a bow and arrows, a couple of daggers and a short Roman sword, "which the young student had bought from a Jew when he was last in Caerleon". The visitor is taken to the student's large wooden hall or college and there sees the sort of subjects that are taught: the Holy Scriptures, the wise sayings of Cadoc of Llancarfan, the art of writing and the illumination of manuscripts, and then the boys' school where 'bright little fellows' are learning the Articles of the Creed and the Ages of the World. When their lessons were finished, "they were free to bound over the green-sward in the meadows, under the shadow of 'Castle Ditches', or ramble on the coast and fling pebbles over the arch in Tryssilion's wave-washed cavern".

The guided tour continues with a visit to the mills, the smithy and the carpenter's shop, then leaves the *vallum* (the stone or earth enclosure around the monastic buildings and school) to see the monastery's farm, with students busy at work "receiving instruction in agriculture and husbandry". The tour concludes with a climb to Castle Ditches to look down "on the great embankment which had been raised to prevent the waters of the Bristol Channel flooding the low-lying meadows". Fryer concludes:

> The sea, the brook, the fields remain, but the ditch, the stone
> wall, the oratories, the populous village of wooden huts, the halls,
> the refectories, and the men and boys who peopled them have
> disappeared ages ago. Still, we are all members of the same family,
> moved by the same passions, influenced by the same affections;
> so let us stretch forth a hand of recognition over the centuries
> that intervene to those who lived, worked, and died in this time-
> honoured place [...] In a sad and dreary age, may we not reckon
> Illtyd, 'the knight', the 'excellent master', as one of the saviours of
> learning and civilization?

Restoration

Following the first restoration of St Illtud's Church in 1888 by G.F. Lambert, a complete restoration was undertaken in 1899 and 1905 by the architects G.E. Halliday, J.W. Roger and A. Caroë. Lambert's work, which included the restoration of the nave walls to reveal the medieval wall paintings, had been severely criticised by the Society for the Protection of Ancient Buildings, mainly because either poor or incorrect material had been used. The 1899 restoration dealt with the West Church and the 1905 restoration with the East Church, including the reredos, and tower.

Significant for the history of St Illtud's was the Cardiff architect George Eley Halliday's painstaking archaeological investigation of the fabric of the church through excavation and the resultant dating of the various parts, which has now become definitive.[243] In his article in *Archaeologia Cambrensis* following the 1905 restoration, Halliday provided plans of what he saw as the Norman church, which is the present West Church with a short extension of the transept and chancel into what is now the East Church. He did admit that it was "a matter of pure conjecture" that this was the rebuilding of a pre-Norman stone church contemporary with the Illtud Cross, which he believed was in its original position on the north side of the churchyard until it was brought into the West Church in 1902. Bones were found under it when it was moved. There was a stone cist containing a skeleton a few inches away alongside, which Halliday proved to have been put in at the same time as the cross.[244] Nash-Williams dated the cross to the late tenth century, whereas Redknap and Lewis preferred the early tenth century. If Halliday's conjecture that the Illtud Cross was erected at the same time as a pre-Norman stone church was built is correct, then this would add weight to the theory that Llanilltud could have relocated from its previous site closer to the coast sometime during the tenth century, possibly following Viking raids and with the rise of royal patronage, with a stone church built where the West Church is now.

Halliday cleared up the confusion over the different parts of the church. Local tradition called the West Church the 'Old Church' and the East Church the 'New Church', which had puzzled some historians as on a cursory investigation, the style of architecture in the West Church appears later than that of the East Church. He exposed the foundations of the Norman building and stripped back wall plaster, showing a line about two feet above ground where the masonry changes from the earlier work to the fifteenth-century rebuilding. His plan of the thirteenth-century church showed clearly the original design of the East Church, with the continuation of the south aisle, and then the plan of the fourteenth- and fifteenth-century alterations with the shortening of the south aisle and the insertion of the reredos. Halliday believed that the Lady Chapel – now called the Galilee Chapel – at the west end, built at the same time as the East Church, was remodelled in the fifteenth century; though as the chapel was roofless and some of the walls lost by the time of his investigation, he did not give it the same careful consideration as he did the rest of the church.

1959 saw further restoration and restructuring at St Illtud's under the architect George Pace, who had overseen the rebuilding of Llandaff Cathedral following its war damage. In 1992 the glass doors between the West and East Church were inserted, and also a spiral staircase into the Parvise Room to enable it to be used as a choir vestry. The wall paintings were also cleaned. Then in 2013 the Galilee Chapel was rebuilt.

The Galilee Chapel

In 1963, the then Vicar of Llantwit Major, Canon Dilwyn Llewellyn Jones, presented his vision for rebuilding and refurbishing the Galilee Chapel to the parish. He was a distinguished historian and the founder-president of the Llantwit Major Local History Society in 1967. Canon Jones' concern was to rescue the history of Llanilltud from the myths that had grown up through the writings of Iolo Morganwg by ensuring that what was presented as history had a factual basis.

However, it was not until the late 1990s that consideration was given to presenting the story of Llanilltud through developing an education centre and rehousing the early medieval stones, which could not be fully appreciated in their position in the West Church. A 'Millennium Project' was drawn up, which would have involved the rebuilding of the Chantry Priest's House as an exhibition and education centre, laying out the Globe field opposite the church as a Celtic Christian monastery, and a board-walk constructed down to the beach as the 'Saints' Way'. This proved too ambitious, so consideration was given to resurrecting Canon Dilwyn Jones' vision of rebuilding the Galilee Chapel, moving the early medieval stones there, and using the former sacristy as a kitchen with an archive room above.

A new project was initiated in 2009 and Michael Davies, then of Davies Sutton Architects, was given the task of drawing up plans for rebuilding the Galilee Chapel as a more suitable setting in which to display the stones and to provide space for those wishing to study the history and spirituality of Llanilltud. Michael Davies' scheme strove to retain the character of a ruin in a finished building, retaining the existing walls and masonry details with simple structural glazing filling the space between the roof and the walls. A new mezzanine floor was introduced above the eastern part of the Galilee Chapel where the original Lady Chapel and Raglan Chantry would have been, providing a viewing area to look down on the stones, space for meetings, and access to the upper floor of the old sacristy for office and archive space.

The work began on 6 September 2012 and was undertaken by the construction firm Knox and Wells. An archaeological survey prior to the construction work revealed skeletal remains and an ossuary, a pit of human bones that were probably deposited there after the restoration of the West Church in 1900. However, while a tenth-century bronze bookmark was discovered, it could not be proved that there was a building on the site that predated the construction of the Galilee Chapel in the thirteenth century.

The work took over a year to complete. The removal of the early medieval stones from the West Church and their resetting in the Galilee Chapel has been described as a remarkable feat of engineering. A photographic survey was made of the stones, which were then cleaned and consolidated to prevent any further deterioration. A scaffold with a six-metre lifting beam was constructed to lift the stones, which were then lowered onto rollers to be moved into the Galilee Chapel. It had to be borne in mind that there was almost as much of each stone below the surface as above, the Illtud Cross measuring 1.8 m from the ground up but 1.2 m from the ground down to the base. The repositioning of the stones in the Chapel allowed them to be viewed from all sides for the first time in over a hundred years.

The restored chapel was opened on 2 November 2013, followed by a celebration of thanksgiving on Sunday 3 November, at which the Most Revd Dr Barry Morgan, Archbishop of Wales, rededicated the Galilee Chapel. He said, "This restoration is magnificent. It is both sensitive to this ancient site in the way it has been restored and yet surprisingly contemporary in its use of light and space. This means it can be a place of pilgrimage and be useable in all kinds of ways by the present church community."

In 2014, architect Michael Davies won the prestigious Welsh Architecture Award from the Royal Institute of British Architects (RIBA) for the conversion of the Galilee Chapel at St Illtud's. The citation explains how the project has been a great contribution to British architecture:

> The Galilee Chapel is the realisation of a dream to restore a ruin which has remained in disrepair for over 400 years, and provide a suitable building to commemorate the cradle of 'Celtic' Christianity in Britain. Even this final solution has been years in gestation, but the patient result fulfils the brief superbly and provides the church with desperately needed space, a suitably reverent area in which to display the ancient Celtic stones and added facilities to give the church further space for its congregation and the local community.
>
> The Chapel provides a new, well lit, calm and dignified stage to exhibit the stones, and also accommodates rest-rooms, a meeting/gallery space, a kitchen and an office. The constraints of

the existing structure have been overcome by the architect through both following conservation principles and being innovative where required. The ruined side walls have been framed in stone and glazed extensively, allowing natural light to flood into the space. From the main body of the church this gives the chapel an almost celestial light through the internal glazed doors which draws visitors in.

Materials such as local stone, lime, natural slates, limewash, natural oak boarding and frameless glazing all give the Chapel a feeling of permanence and quality which allow it to sit well next to the existing church, but not to hide its more contemporary detailing. The jury felt this was a confident solution to a difficult brief. Despite the restrictions imposed by the existing structure, the fact this is consecrated ground, disability access issues and archaeological concerns, the architect has produced a design of quality, and delivered a building which is well-detailed throughout and with no little panache. It shows a high level of maturity and confidence in terms of conservation design.

The project was funded by the Heritage Lottery Fund, Cadw, the Vale of Glamorgan Borough Council, other grant-making bodies and private donations, and through fundraising by the church. It is marketed as Llanilltud and receives many visitors from the UK and overseas. On 1 July 2014, what is believed to be the first royal visit to St Illtud's Church took place, when HRH The Prince of Wales and the Duchess of Cornwall were welcomed to the church by the rector, the Revd Huw Butler, and introduced to the Galilee Chapel project. They met the architect and those directly involved with the project, along with local parishioners and schoolchildren, and were shown around the Chapel.

The restored Galilee Chapel, the sensitive display of the early medieval stones, and the interpretative panels ensure that the memory of Llanilltud will be kept alive for future generations. The vision of Llanilltud becoming another Iona or Lindisfarne may be ambitious, but it is as significant in the history of Christianity in Wales as they are in the history of Scotland or the north of England.

153

BIBLIOGRAPHY

ALCOCK, Leslie, *Dinas Powys: An Iron Age, Dark Age and Early Medieval Settlement in Glamorgan* (University of Wales Press, 1963)

BEDE, *Ecclesiastical History of the English People*, translated by Leo Sherley-Price (Penguin Books, 1990)

BOWEN, E.G., *Saints, Seaways and Settlements* (University of Wales Press, 1977)

CHARLES-EDWARDS, T.M., *Wales and the Britons 350–1064* (Oxford University Press, 2013)

CUNLIFFE, Barry, and KOCH, John (eds.), *Celtic from the West: Alternative Perspectives from Archaeology, Genetics, Language and Literature* (Oxbow Books, 2010)

DAVIES, John Reuben, *The Book of Llandaff and the Norman Church in Wales* (Boydell Press, 2003)

DAVIES, Oliver and BOWIE, Fiona, *Celtic Christian Spirituality* (SPCK, 1995)

DAVIES, Wendy, *The Llandaff Charters* (National Library of Wales, 1980)

DOBLE, G.H., *Lives of the Welsh Saints* (University of Wales Press, 1971)

EVANS, C.J., *Glamorgan, its History and Topography* (William Lewis, 1938)

EVANS, D. Simon (ed.), *The Welsh Life of St David* (University of Wales Press, 1988)

FOX, Cyril, *Life and Death in the Bronze Age: An Archaeologist's Field-work* (Routledge, 1959)

154

FREEMAN, Philip, *The World of St Patrick* (Oxford University Press, 2014)

FRYER, Alfred, *Llantwit Major: A Fifth-Century University* (Elliot Stock, 1893)

GILDAS, *De Excidio et Conquestu Britanniae*, translated by J.A. Giles as *On the Ruin of Britain: De Excidio Britanniae* (Serenity Publishers, 2009)

GIRALDUS CAMBRENSIS (Gerald of Wales), *The Journey through Wales and The Description of Wales*, translated by Lewis Thorpe (Penguin Books, 1978)

GREEN, C.A., *Notes on Churches in the Diocese of Llandaff*, 1906.

HALLIDAY, George E., 'Llantwit Major Church, Glamorgan' in *Archaeologia Cambrensis*, 1900.

HALLIDAY, George E., 'Llantwit Major Church, Glamorgan' in *Archaeologia Cambrensis*, 1905.

HARDINGE, Leslie, *The Celtic Church in Britain* (SPCK, 1972)

HERREN, Michael W. and BROWN, Shirley Ann, *Christ in Celtic Christianity* (Boydell Press, 2002)

JENKINS, Simon, *Wales: Churches, Houses, Castles* (Allen Lane, 2008)

KNIGHT, Jeremy, *South Wales from the Romans to the Normans* (Amberley Publishing, 2013)

MALKIN, Benjamin Heath, *The Scenery, Antiquities and Biography of South Wales* (Longman and Rees, 1804, reprinted by S.R. Publishers Ltd, 1970)

MORGANS, John and NOBLE, Peter, *Our Holy Ground* (Y Lolfa, 2016)

NEWMAN, John, *The Buildings of Wales: Glamorgan* (Penguin Books & University of Wales Press, 1995)

OLSON, Lynette (ed.), *St Samson of Dol and the Earliest History of Brittany, Cornwall and Wales* (Boydell Press, 2017)

ORRIN, Geoffrey R., *Medieval Churches of the Vale of Glamorgan* (D. Brown and Sons Ltd, 1988)

PENNAR, Meirion (trans.), *The Black Book of Carmarthen* (Llanerch Enterprises, 1989)

PETTS, David, *The Early Medieval Church in Wales* (The History Press, 2009)

REDKNAP, Mark and LEWIS, John, *A Corpus of Early Medieval Inscribed Stones and Stone Sculpture in Wales*, Vol. 1 (University of Wales Press, 2007)

RODGER, John W., 'The Ecclesiastical Buildings of Llantwit Major', in *Transactions of the Cardiff Naturalists Society*, 1906.

ROBERTS, Alice, *The Celts: Search for a Civilisation* (Heron Books, 2015)

STEPHEN, Ray, 'The Excavation at Caer Mead 1888', in *Llantwit Major Aspects of its History*, Vol. 4 (Llantwit Major Local History Society).

TAYLOR, Thomas (trans.), *Vita Samsonis* (SPCK, 1925)

THOMAS, Charles, *Celtic Britain* (Thames and Hudson, 1986)

THOMAS, Charles, *Britain and Ireland in Early Christian Times* (Thames and Hudson, 1971)

THOMAS, Hilary M., *History in Stones* (privately published, 2013)

THOMAS, Lawrence, *The Reformation in the Old Diocese of Llandaff* (William Lewis Printers, 1930)

THOMAS, Patrick, *Candle in the Darkness* (Gomer Press, 1993)

THURLBY, Malcolm, *Romanesque Architecture and Sculpture in Wales* (Logaston Press, 2006)

TREVELYAN, Marie, *Llantwit Major, its History and Antiquities* (John E. Southall, 1910)

WILLIAMS, Glanmor, *The Welsh Church from Conquest to Reformation* (University of Wales Press, 1962)

WILLIAMS, Taliesin (trans.), *Iolo Manuscripts – a selection of ancient Welsh manuscripts* (Welsh MSS Society, 1848)

ENDNOTES

Introduction

[1] R.S. Thomas, *Collected Poems 1945–1990* (Phoenix, 2000), p.282.

[2] Rice Merrick, *A Booke of Glamorganshires Antiquities*, edited by James Andrew Corbett (Dryden Press 1887, reprinted by Stewart Williams, 1972).

[3] Benjamin Heath Malkin, *The Scenery, Antiquities and Biography of South Wales*.

[4] http://www.catholic.org/saints/saint.php?saint_id=3848

[5] Taliesin Williams (trans.), *Iolo Manuscripts – a selection of ancient Welsh manuscripts*.

[6] *The Guardian*, 28 March 2014.

[7] Centre for Economics and Business Research press release, August 26, 2014.

[8] C.J. Evans, *Glamorgan, its History and Topography*, p.310.

[9] Recorded in Marie Trevelyan, *Llantwit Major, its History and Antiquities*, p.22.

[10] The leaflet *Llanilltud – the Galilee Chapel* (St Illtud's Church, 2013).

[11] Simon Jenkins, *Wales Churches, Houses, Castles*, p.158.

Chapter 1: Llanilltud before St Illtud

[12] See Cyril Fox, *Life and Death in the Bronze Age: An Archaeologist's Field-work*.

[13] Tacitus, *Annales* Xi.ii.

[14] See Barry Cunliffe and John Koch, eds., *Celtic from the West: Alternative Perspectives from Archaeology, Genetics, Language and Literature*. This book is based on a forum, 'Celticisation from the West', held at the National Library

of Wales, Aberystwyth in December 2008. This hypothesis is explored in a more accessible form by Alice Roberts in *The Celts: Search for a Civilisation*.

[15] See Ray Stephen, *The Excavation at Caer Mead 1888* in *Llantwit Major Aspects of its History*, Vol. 4. A full report of the excavations is to be found in the *Report and Transactions of the Cardiff Naturalists' Society*, Vol. XX, Part II, 1888.

[16] Gildas, *De Excidio et Conquestu Britanniae*, IIx.

[17] Bede, *Ecclesiastical History of the English People*, p.54. The footnote identifies the City of Legions as possibly being Caerleon.

[18] Thomas Taylor (trans.), *Vita Samsonis* I.XIII.

[19] *ibid.* I.XLIV.

[20] Taylor, introduction to *ibid.*, p.xi.

[21] *Vita Iltuti Abbatis VI* (twelfth century).

[22] See T.M. Charles-Edwards, *Wales and the Britons 350–1064*, p.194.

[23] Bede, *Ecclesiastical History of the English People* I.17.

[24] *ibid.* I.20.

[25] *ibid.* I.21.

[26] *Vita Sancti David* XLIX.

[27] *ibid.* LII.

[28] *Vita Samsonis* I.XLII.

[29] *ibid.* I.VII.

[30] See E.G. Bowen, *Saints, Seaways and Settlements*, p.66.

[31] See Leslie Alcock, *Dinas Powys: an Iron Age, Dark Age and Early Medieval Settlement in Glamorgan*, 1963.

[32] Giraldus Cambrensis (Gerald of Wales), *The Journey through Wales and The Description of Wales*, p.253.

[33] Muirchú, 'Life of St Patrick' in Philip Freeman, *The World of St Patrick*, p.62.

[34] 'Confessions of St Patrick' in *ibid.*, p.30.

Chapter 2: The Life of St Illtud

[35] The most useful English translation of the complete text can be found at http://www.maryjones.us/ctexts/illtud.html,

though G.H. Doble in *Lives of the Welsh Saints*, p.197ff., provides a translation of the more important passages.

36   Taylor, *Vita Samsonis*.

37   Thomas Taylor, *ibid.*, writing in 1925, claims a date between 610–615. Pierre Flobert in his French translation, *La Vie ancienne de saint Samson de Dol* (CNRS Editions, 1997) believes the *Vita Samsonis* to have been written much later, in the eighth century, on the basis that the author knew the works of the Venerable Bede. T.M. Charles-Edwards in *Wales and the Britons 350–1064* favours the early date because of the use of particular geographical names that would not be possible after the seventh century (see p.238f.) and also on linguistic grounds (p.625). The most recent study, Lynette Olson (ed.), *St Samson of Dol and the Earliest History of Brittany, Cornwall and Wales,* suggests a later seventh-century date for the *Vita Samsonis*, but posits that there was a previous Life on which the author drew.

38   Eltut is an early Welsh form of Illtud.

39   *Vita Samsonis* I.VII.

40   Taylor, *ibid.*, p.14.

41   *ibid.*, I.XLII.

42   Taylor, *ibid.*, p.xi.

43   *ibid.* I.VI, I.VII.

44   *ibid.* I.VII.

45   *ibid.* I.VIII.

46   Sabine Baring-Gould and John Fisher, *Lives of the British Saints* (first published 1907–1911; edited by Derek Bryce and reprinted by Llanerch Enterprises, 1990).

47   Adrian Geoffrey Gilbert, Alan Wilson and Baram Blackett, *The Holy Kingdom: Quest for the Real King Arthur* (Corgi Books, 1999).

48   Chris Barber, *King Arthur: The Mystery Unravelled* (Pen & Sword History, 2016).

49   *Vita Iltuti* II.

50   *ibid.* I.

51   *ibid.* II.

52 *Vita Cadoci* XVI.

53 *Vita Iltuti* III.

54 *ibid.* VI.

55 *ibid.* XVI.

56 *Vita Pauli Aureliani* III.

57 The Bristol Channel has the second highest tidal range in the world, exceeded only by the Bay of Fundy in Canada.

58 *Vita Iltuti* XIII.

59 *ibid.* XIX.

60 *ibid.* XXIV.

61 6 November, still observed as St Illtud's festival day.

62 *Vita Iltuti* XXIV.

63 *Vita Samsonis* I.VII.

Chapter 3: Llanilltud in the sixth century

64 Bede, *Ecclesiastical History of the English People* I.23.

65 *Vita Iltuti* VII.

66 *ibid.* VI.

67 *ibid.* X.

68 *ibid.* XXVI.

69 Marie Trevelyan, writing in 1910 in *Llantwit Major, its History and Antiquities,* said that the piles and supports of a pier, to be seen at a very low tide, are called locally 'The Black Men'. A survey undertaken at that time showed that on one side of the timber piles the stones are laid "with great regularity, and the excellent masonry is as strong as ever."

70 Lucy Toulmin Smith (ed.), *The Itinerary of John Leland.* Vol. III. part VI (George Bell and Sons, 1906).

71 For an analysis of the port at the mouth of the Colhuw, see P. Davies and A.T. Williams' 'The enigma of the destruction of Colhuw Port, Wales' in *The Geographic Review,* Vol. 81, No. 3, 1991.

72 *Vita Iltuti* XIII.

73 Quoted in G.H. Doble, *Lives of the Welsh Saints* p.94f.

74 Marie Trevelyan in *Llantwit Major, its History and Antiquities* records storm surges in 255, 351, 353, 414 and 500, as well

as later. In 1483, a flood called 'Buckingham's storm' is said to have almost overwhelmed the ports of Aberthaw, Llantwit Major, Candleston and Kenfig.

75 *Archaeologia Cambrensis*, Series 6, No. III, January 1903, p.56ff.

76 See the Llanilltud website: www.llanilltud.org.uk

77 John Morgans and Peter Noble, *Our Holy Ground*, p.27.

78 *Vita Samsonis* I.VII.

79 *Vita Iltuti* I.

80 *Vita Samsonis* I.VII.

81 *ibid.* I.V.

82 *ibid.* I.VI, I.VII.

83 *ibid.* I.IX.

84 *Vita Iltuti* X.

85 *Vita Samsonis* I.X.

86 *ibid.* I.XI.

87 *ibid.* I.XXXXIV.

88 *ibid.* I.XXXVIII. While the *Vita Samsonis* does not name the monastery, the footnote in Thomas Taylor's translation identifies it as Dun Etair, on the promontory of Howth, north of Dublin.

89 *ibid.* I.XLV.

90 Quoted in Doble, *Lives of the Welsh Saints*, p.94.

91 Rhygyfarch, *Vita Sancti David* X.

92 *ibid.* LXVI.

93 *ibid.* XLVI.

94 D. Simon Evans (ed.), *The Welsh Life of St David*, p.13.

95 Gildas, *De Excidio et Conquestu Britanniae* XXVI. Charles Thomas in *Celtic Britain* suggests Badon Hill is Liddington Castle, south of Swindon, Wiltshire.

96 Bede, *Ecclesiastical History* I.16.

97 Hugh Williams (trans.), *Vita Gildae* III (Llanerch Publishers, 1990).

98 *ibid.* IV.

99 *ibid.* V.

100 *Vita Samsonis* I.XV: Samson "took his meals daily with the

rest of the brothers".

[101] *The Book of Kells,* fo. 202v, illustrating the Temptation of Christ from St Luke's Gospel.

[102] *Vita Iltuti* XVIII.

[103] *ibid.* XIX.

[104] *ibid.* XXV.

[105] *ibid.* X.

[106] *Vita Samsonis* I.VII.

[107] *ibid.* I.XLII.

[108] *Vita S. Dubricii* IV.

[109] Bede, *Ecclesiastical History* IV.4.

[110] *Vita Samsonis* I.I.

[111] *ibid.* I.XIV.

[112] *ibid.* I.XVI.

[113] *ibid.* I.XVIII.

[114] *ibid.* I.XIX.

[115] *ibid.* I.XLII.

[116] Published by Darton, Longman and Todd, 1988.

[117] e.g. *The Edge of Glory: Collection of modern prayers in the Celtic tradition; The Open Gate: Celtic-style prayers for spiritual growth; The Rhythm of Life: Morning, Midday, Evening and Night liturgies for each day of the week; Tides and Seasons: A further collection of modern prayers in the Celtic tradition,* all published by SPCK.

[118] *Vita Samsonis* I.XX.

[119] *ibid.* I.VI.

[120] *ibid.* I.X.

[121] *ibid.* I.XIV.

[122] *ibid.* I.XIII.

[123] *ibid.* I.XV.

[124] *ibid.* I.XX.

[125] *ibid.* I.XXI.

[126] *ibid.* I.XXXVI.

[127] *ibid.* I.VIII.

[128] *ibid.* I.XIII.

[129] *ibid.* "the morsel": I.XVIII; "the chalice": I.XIII.

130 *ibid.* I.XLV.

131 *ibid.* I.XXXIII.

132 *ibid.* II.XII.

133 *ibid.* I.XIX.

134 *ibid.* I.XLII.

135 Matthew 16:13–20.

136 *Vita Samsonis* I.XLIII.

137 *ibid.* II.II; St Samson's festival day is 28 July.

138 *ibid.* II.V.

139 *ibid.* II.XVI.

140 *ibid.* I.XIII.

141 *ibid.* I.XLIV.

142 *Vita Sancti David* XXI–XXVI.

143 *Vita Iltuti* X.

144 Malkin, *The Scenery, Antiquities and Biography of South Wales*, p.619.

145 *Vita Iltuti* VIII.

146 See examples in Oliver Davies and Fiona Bowie, *Celtic Christian Spirituality*.

147 *Vita Iltuti* XIII.

148 *ibid.* XI, quoting Matthew 25:31–45.

149 *Vita Samsonis* I.XV.

150 *ibid.* I.XXII, XXIII.

151 *ibid.* I.XXV.

152 *ibid.* I.XLV.

153 *ibid.* I.XLV.

154 *ibid.* I.XLVI.

155 *ibid.* I.LI.

156 *Vita Iltuti* XVIII.

157 *ibid.* XXI.

158 *Vita Samsonis* I.XLVII.

159 *Vita Sancti David* XV.

Chapter 4: Llanilltud from the seventh to eleventh century

160 Gildas, *De Excidio et Conquestu Britanniae* III.65.

161 *ibid.* III.66.

[162] Bede, *Ecclesiastical History* II.2.

[163] *ibid.* II.2.

[164] See John Reuben Davies, *The Book of Llandaff and the Norman Church in Wales*, p.89f.

[165] David Nichols, 'The Antiquities of Lantwit Major', written in 1729, is found as an appendix to David Williams' *The History of Monmouthshire* (H. Baldwin, 1796). Cited in *The Book of Llandaff and the Norman Church in Wales*, p.14.

[166] From the list compiled by Chancellor J.W. James and R.W.D. Fenn in the various editions of *The Llandaff Diocesan Handbook*.

[167] e.g. in the *Vita Cadoci* LV.

[168] e.g. by Chris Barber in *King Arthur: The Mystery Unravelled*, p.114.

[169] See Mark Redknap and John Lewis, *A Corpus of Early Medieval Inscribed Stones and Stone Sculpture in Wales*, Vol. 1, p.390ff.

[170] Malcolm Thurlby, *Romanesque Architecture and Sculpture in Wales*, p.71f.

[171] Redknap and Lewis, *A Corpus of Early Medieval Inscribed Stones and Stone Sculpture in Wales*, p.380.

[172] The term 'Herefordshire School of Sculpture' was first used by George Zarnecki in an unpublished PhD thesis in 1951, to refer to what he believed was a group of master masons working in the county and those neighbouring it in the twelfth century. He identified common key features in sculpture in many of the Norman churches in the area which are not found elsewhere.

[173] T.M. Charles-Edwards, *Wales and the Britons*, p.626ff.

[174] *ibid.*, p.631.

[175] *Vita Iltuti* X.

[176] Walter de Gray Birch, *Memorials of Llandaff Cathedral* (John E. Richards, 1912), p.99.

[177] *Vita Iltuti* X.

[178] See *ibid.* XV, where a spring was given Samson's name.

[179] In Davies and Bowie, *Celtic Christian Spirituality*.

[180] Meirion Pennar (trans.), *The Black Book of Carmarthen*, p.59.

[181] *ibid.*, p.55.

[182] Translation from Oliver Davies, *Celtic Christian Spirituality in Early Medieval Wales* (University of Wales Press, 1996), p.50f. A facsimile with introductory notes by Myriah Williams can be seen at https://cudl.lib.cam.ac.uk/view/MS-FF-00004-00042/1

[183] See Michael W. Herren and Shirley Ann Brown, *Christ in Celtic Christianity*, p.189ff, 205.

[184] e.g. *Pange Lingua Gloriosi Proelium Certaminis* (Sing my tongue the glorious battle) and *Vexilla Regis prodeunt* (The royal banners forward go; the Cross shines forth in mystic glow).

Chapter 5: Llanilltud and the Norman Conquest

[185] *Vita Iltuti* XXVI.

[186] C.A. Green, *Notes on Churches in the Diocese of Llandaff*, part 2, p.33.

[187] *Vita Iltuti* XII.

[188] *Vita Cadoci* XLVIII.

[189] John Reuben Davies, *The Book of Llandaff and the Norman Church in Wales*, p.57.

[190] Green, *Notes on Churches in the Diocese of Llandaff*, part 2, p.33f.

[191] *ibid.*, part 2, p.34.

[192] *ibid.*, part 2, p.35.

[193] *Dictionary of National Biography, 1885–1900* (Oxford University Press).

[194] See the article by George E. Halliday, the architect of the 1899–1905 restoration, in *Archaeologia Cambrensis* Series 6, Vol. 5 (1905), pp.242–250. Halliday implies that the foundations of the West Church were those of a pre-Norman building, but in a previous article (*Archaeologia Cambrensis* Series 5, Vol. 17 (1900), pp.129–156) he suggests that they are early Norman.

[195] Thurlby, *Romanesque Architecture and Sculpture in Wales*, p.71ff.

[196] Giraldus Cambrensis (Gerald of Wales), *The Journey through Wales and The Description of Wales*, p.88.

[197] *Vita Iltuti* XXIII.

[198] *ibid.* XVI.

[199] Quoted in Doble, *Lives of the Welsh Saints*, p.100.

[200] Quoted in *ibid.*, p.140.

[201] Redknap and Lewis, *A Corpus of Early Medieval Inscribed Stones and Stone Sculpture in Wales*, p.366.

[202] *ibid.*, p.367.

[203] *ibid.*, p.363.

[204] Thurlby, *Romanesque Architecture and Sculpture in Wales*, p.67ff.

[205] *ibid.*, p.210.

Chapter 6: Llanilltud from the thirteenth century to the Reformation

[206] John Newman, *The Buildings of Wales: Glamorgan*, p.407.

[207] V.E. Nash-Williams, *The Medieval Settlement at Llantwit Major Glamorgan* (University of Wales Press, reprinted from the *Bulletin of the Board of Celtic Studies*, Vol. XIV, Part IV, 1952), pp.313–333.

[208] Green, *Notes on Churches in the Diocese of Llandaff*, p.55.

[209] Rodger, 'The Ecclesiastical Buildings of Llantwit Major', p.31.

[210] *ibid.*, p.27.

[211] David Nichols, 'The Antiquities of Lantwit Major', in the appendix to David Williams, *The History of Monmouthshire*, p.46.

[212] Nash-Williams, *The Medieval Settlement at Llantwit Major Glamorgan*.

[213] Cited in Rodger, 'The Ecclesiastical Buildings of Llantwit Major', p.46f.

[214] From the Tewkesbury Abbey Ministers Accounts 1449–50, cited in Hilary M. Thomas, *History in Stones*, p.10.

215 Feffes = feoffees: "A trustee invested with a freehold estate in land" (*Oxford English Dictionary*).

216 Rodger, 'The Ecclesiastical Buildings of Llantwit Major', p.32ff.

217 Lawrence Thomas, *The Reformation in the Old Diocese of Llandaff*, p.15.

218 *ibid.*, p.106.

Chapter 7: Keeping the memory of Llanilltud alive, seventeenth to twenty-first century

219 Somerset.

220 Taliesin Williams, *Iolo Manuscripts*, p.343f.

221 *ibid.*, p.422.

222 *ibid.*, p.353.

223 *ibid.*, p.533.

224 *ibid.*, p.534.

225 *ibid.*, p.455.

226 *ibid.*, p.534f.

227 *ibid.*, p.555.

228 *ibid.*, p.363.

229 *ibid.*, p.364.

230 See Brian Davies, 'Iolo and the Samson Pillar', in *Llantwit Major: Aspects of its History*, Vol. 9, 2009, p.5ff.

231 Redknap and Lewis, *A Corpus of Early Medieval Inscribed Stones and Stone Sculpture in Wales*, p.381f.

232 Brian Davies, 'Iolo and the Samson Pillar', p.10.

233 Redknap and Lewis, *A Corpus of Early Medieval Inscribed Stones and Stone Sculpture in Wales*, p.13.

234 Malkin, *The Scenery, Antiquities and Biography of South Wales*, p.618.

235 *Archaeologia Cambrensis*, No. XIII, January 1849, p.18f.

236 *Archaeologia Cambrensis*, No. XVI, October 1849, p.326.

237 Redknap and Lewis, *A Corpus of Early Medieval Inscribed Stones and Stone Sculpture in Wales*, p.15.

238 *Archaeologia Cambrensis*, Third Series, No. XIII, January 1858, p.31ff.

[239] *ibid.*, p.42ff.

[240] *ibid.*, p.47.

[241] *Archaeologia Cambrensis*, No. XVI, October 1849, p.303.

[242] Alfred Fryer, *Llantwit Major: A Fifth-Century University*, p.68.

[243] e.g. in John Newman, *The Buildings of Wales: Glamorgan* and Geoffrey R. Orrin, *Medieval Churches of the Vale of Glamorgan*.

[244] *Archaeologia Cambrensis*, Series 6, No. III, January 1903, p.56ff.

Index

Also from Y Lolfa:

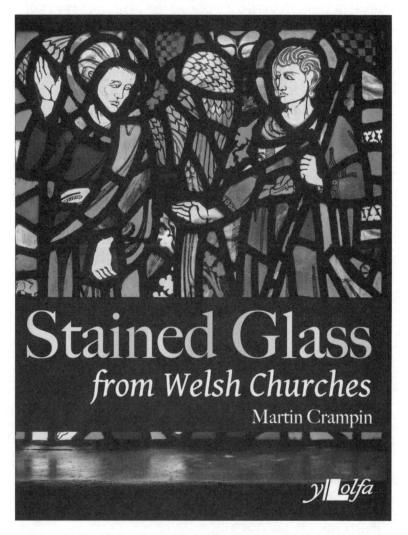

£29.95 (hb)

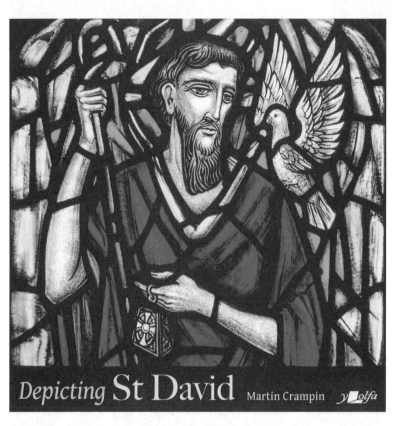

Depicting St David Martin Crampin *y Lolfa*

£7.99

In Pursuit of
SAINT
DAVID
PATRON SAINT OF WALES

Gerald Morgan   y Lolfa

£5.99